Flying Low

Flying Low

Steven E. Blanton

Deeds Publishing | Athens

Published by Deeds Publishing in Athens, GA
www.deedspublishing.com

Printed in The United States of America

Cover design by Mark Babcock. Text layout by Matt King.

ISBN 978-1-947309-60-9

Books are available in quantity for promotional or premium use. For information, email info@deedspublishing.com.

First Edition, 2019

10 9 8 7 6 5 4 3 2 1

DEDICATION

This was the easy part of my book project. After finishing the majority of the chapters I began to think that in order to be a real book I should dedicate this work to someone. Well, it was no contest. I proudly dedicate this book to my loving wife Gerann. As of 6 June 2019 we will be married 49 years. We've been together since February 1968 when we met in Biology Lab at North Georgia College.

The Lord has blessed our life together in so many ways. Gerann has always supported me in my career and though we haven't always agreed on major decisions, she's always been there for me.

No doubt one of the greatest gifts she ever gave me was in the form of an ultimatum. In August of 1974, I ended my active duty in the Army and we moved to Rutledge, Georgia where we took jobs at the tiny private school, Rutledge Academy. After settling into our new duplex apartment she informed me one Sunday morning that she was going to church. I protested and said something like, "Why do you want to do that?" She put her foot down and said, "Well that's what I want to do and you can either go with me or sit here, but I'm going!" She was good to her word and continued to attend Rutledge Baptist Church by herself for a number of weeks. I don't remember exactly when but finally one Sunday morning I got up and began to get ready. She asked, "What are you doing?" My somewhat unenthusiastic reply was, "I guess I'm going to church with you."

Time rolled along and our first son Chris was born on 22 May 1976. Our Pastor, Bill Alexander, came to visit one evening shortly after we brought Chris home from the hospital. I had been sitting under Brother Bill's preaching for some time and had actually considered making a move but the devil was working hard to keep me from committing. Brother Bill stated that the main purpose of his visit was to ask about arranging a dedication service for Chris on an upcoming Sunday Morning. He asked me, "Don't you want to dedicate Chris to The Lord?" I replied, "Yes, of course I do." Well, that was the opening for Brother Bill's reply that went straight to my heart. He said, "Steve, how can you dedicate your new born son to The Lord when you are not dedicated to The Lord?" That's all it took. I knelt with Brother Bill at the foot of my bed and asked Jesus to come into my heart and save me! I've never looked back and that was truly the most important event in my life and I know that Gerann uttered many prayers on my behalf before that glorious evening, and many since as well.

God has truly blessed our life together. He has given us four beautiful children and nine adorable grandchildren. We also have been blessed to have numerous close friends over the years, an awesome Church Family and we are blessed with relative good health. We have a beautiful home and God is good!

Regarding those *close* friends it's dangerous to start naming them because invariably you'll forget someone. However, I think it is important so here goes: My best friend during my "growing up" years was Chris Walker whom we named our first born son after. Chris Walker met an untimely death just one week after Gerann and I married and I still miss him even today.

James and Danny Bobo, Howard Buice, and I were best buddies in the old neighborhood back in Atlanta. We had several adventures together through our high school years as well.

Larry Fenley and I were close friends through my last two years of high school and we continued to keep in touch throughout our college years. Larry went to the University of Georgia on a track scholarship and I would often visit him in Athens during my four years at NGC. Larry spent several years in the Air Force and flew C-141s.

David Bailey and I have been close friends for over 50 years now. We met during "Frog Week" at NGC in the fall of 1966. His dad, Colonel Jack Bailey, administered the oath of office to both David and me when we were commissioned in May of 1970 at NGC. We have shared many good times together over the years and I treasure his friendship. David is and always has been one of my closest friends and confidant. In fact, you'll probably see David's name in several places throughout this book. I have asked David to write one of the two forewords to this book.

Randell Cline is also a close friend that I've known for over 50 years. We also met at NGC during our Freshman Year. I have many fond memories of Randell and his first wife Margaret double dating with Gerann and me. I would be remiss if I didn't mention Randell's Aunt Rosie and Uncle John; I can close my eyes and still taste that wonderful spaghetti that Aunt Rosie made from scratch!

John Broderick is a fellow classmate from my NGC days. We didn't know each other that well back in our college years. However, in recent years John has become a good friend through our annual golf outings. Each year David, Randell, John, and I travel to Dan and Margaret's lake house on Clark Hill Reservoir. Margaret is David's sister and she and Dan are kind enough to let us use their beautiful lake house as our headquarters for a three to four day golf outing.

I met Tim Reed in 1975 after Gerann and I moved to Rutledge, Georgia when I separated from the Army. Tim helped me as volunteer coach at Rutledge Academy and we quickly became close friends. Over the years Gerann and I have been as close to Tim, Caren, and their family as our own and we value their friendship. We have seen one another through some trying times, the most difficult being when their son Ty was tragically killed in March of 1993. I have asked Tim to write one of the two forewords to this book.

Richard Turk and his family moved to Rutledge in the early 80s. Richard, his wife Linda, Gerann and I, had some great times together going on trips with our two families and with the "Rutledge Opry Club" and sharing special occasions with each other's family. Richard was an encourager and one of my best cheerleaders. He went home to be with The Lord on December 25, 2010. I miss him.

Lindsey and Elaine Partain have been close friends since the middle 80s. Lindsey Partain was and is as good a friend as anyone could ever hope to have. Lindsey and I made several trips together individually and with the Rutledge Opry Club. He loved people and was the eternal optimist. Lindsey was the kind of friend you could call on anytime and he'd be there. Lindsey went home to be with the Lord on January 15, 2015. I miss him every day.

Wayne Henson was my golfing buddy; you can learn quite a bit about someone when you spend four to five hours with them on a golf course. Wayne and I played numerous rounds of golf together. He and Millie went on several trips with our "Rutledge Opry Club". Wayne went home to be with The Lord in July of 2010 and I sorely miss him.

Charles and Bobbie Melton: I met Charles over 20 years ago in the early 90s when Jerry Bolton invited him to play a round of golf with us. We have grown close over these many years and we have shared good times and bad times. One of those bad times occurred in January 2014 when Bobbie suffered a crippling stroke. After three and one half years Bobbie went home to be with The Lord on July 8, 2017. Charles is one of my dearest friends. He is one of those you can call on anytime for anything.

Myron and Mary Frances Threadgill lived across the street from Rutledge Baptist Church. Their son William and our son Ben grew up together. Myron and I worked together with Royal Ambassadors at Rutledge Baptist Church and we served together on the Rutledge City Council. About 30 years ago, Myron and his family moved away to Hoschton, Georgia so they could be near Myron's Mother. Even with this separation we've stayed close through the years. Myron and Mary Frances are dear friends and we have shared many meals, trips, and events with them.

Tom and Vickie Arnold live in Hooker, Oklahoma. Tom is the owner/operator of a large farm there in the panhandle of Oklahoma. I met Tom back in 1970 at Fort Eustis. We were together throughout Transportation Officer Basic Course (TOBC), Flight School, Cobra Transition, Aircraft Maintenance Officer Course (AMOC) and we went to Vietnam on the same airplane in August of 1972. During our time together in the Army, Tom and Vickie were some of our closest friends. The Blantons, Arnolds, Kings, and Hirschs were inseparable. Even though we rarely see Tom and Vickie, we've remained close throughout the years and I count them in the circle of our dearest friends.

Gary King and his wife Joyce live in Etowah, North Carolina. Gary and I went through all our training together as well (see Tom Arnold above). Additionally, Gary and I were also classmates at NGC and we were in ROTC Flight Training together where we earned our Private Pilot's License. Gary and I were also on the same flight home from Vietnam. While in Vietnam our wives, Gerann and Judy (Gary's first wife) shared a rental house together near Atlanta, Georgia. Gary and I lost contact with each other for several years. However, we've reconnected during the last 10-15 years and I count Gary as one of my dear friends.

John and Cheryl Hirsch live in Sioux Falls, South Dakota. John and I were together through all our military training (see Tom Arnold). We too lost contact for several years. However, we have remained close throughout the years because of that special bond we all share through our military careers. We visited John and Cheryl in South Dakota along with Tom and Vickie in July of 2011. The six of us had a wonderful time reenergizing friendships that remain close to this day. In October of 2017, the Hirschs, Arnolds, Kings, and several of our other classmates from Flight Class 71-44 met in Nashville, Tennessee for a Reunion. It was if we'd just been apart for a few weeks rather than over 40 years. We all had a great time sharing stories from many years ago, along with catching up regarding family, careers, and life experiences in general.

There have been many others who have supported me and my family, loved us and helped us. Here are a few: Tom and Deanna Owensby, Frances Thompson, Ray Rousseau, Jimmy Thompson, Mike Huff, Bobby Gene and Betty Conner, Betty Jean Hensler, Mary Sauls, Jerry and Phyllis Bolton, Russell and Nina Smith, Alvin Scott, Greg Edwards, Tom Jaynes, Stu Drake, Leslie Groover, Robert Tadlock, Ralph Allen, Danny Stone, Phillip Stephens, David Young, Ken Woods, Steve Reece, Jay Hamilton, Paul Jones, Reid Callaway, Jim Crupi and Bob Stein just to name a few. We have been blessed with many friends throughout the years too numerous to mention all by name. Gerann and I are thankful for each of them.

Of course my Pastors at Rutledge Baptist Church have been special in our life. Bill Alexander led me to a saving knowledge of The Lord and baptized me. Ronnie Wheeless baptized our two oldest sons, Chris and Jesse, ordained me as a Deacon in 1981 and recommended me to be a Gideon in 1985. Bobby Bradley baptized our two youngest children, Ben and Stephanie. Wayne Ghann has been our Pastor for 26 years and performed the marriage ceremony for our daughter Stephanie and her husband Patrick. His ministry has led our Church to be more loving and mission minded. I have grown spiritually under his ministry.

Christopher Wade Blanton is our first born. He arrived on 22 May 1976. We named him after my boyhood friend Chris Walker. Our Chris has been a blessing to us. His love of music and the enormous talent God has bestowed on him has been a point of pride for Gerann and me his entire life. When he had his sixth birthday I started calling him "Big Six" and to this day I often refer to him by that name. At this writing he is now 43 years old! He married Laura Millirons on 29 July 2000; they have five children, Stephen James, Abigail Grace, Samuel Thomas, Alexander Eli, and Victoria Rose. Victoria was born on 17 February 2017; she is our youngest grandbaby; that makes nine! Chris is currently the Minister of Music at Winder First Baptist Church.

Jesse Anderson Blanton was born 12 October 1977; he couldn't wait to get here so he arrived six weeks early! Consequently, he weighed just 3 lbs 8 oz! Early on, I began calling him "Bones" because there just wasn't much more than bones to his little body. I still refer to him by that nickname even though he has more than caught up for his slow start. Early on Jesse showed an interest in running and I cherish the memories of literally taking him all over the country running Junior Olympic Cross Country and Track. He pursued his running through-out high school and college and even today at over 40 years old he and his wife Robin both love running. He married Robin Carver on 17 January 2003; they have three children, Lauren Marie, Joshua Thomas, and Georgia Elise. Jesse is a combat veteran of three tours in Iraq and two in Afghanistan; he is currently a Lieutenant Colonel. He and his family are in Germany where Jesse is assigned as the Aviation Officer for U.S. Army Europe.

Benjamin Dee Blanton was born on 4 October 1982; he was our biggest baby at over 8 pounds! We sometimes call him "Ben-Ben"! We are very proud of Ben; he is our "prodigal son"! Ben "lost his way" for several years but The Lord brought him back! Ben moved back home when he was in his early twenties. Since then he has gone back to school and earned a degree in Business Management from Terry Business College at the University of Georgia, he has been actively involved in his Church, Royal Diadem Tabernacle, and has been on several mission trips. Ben became a homeowner in June of 2015. Ben and Sarah Elizabeth Yawn were married on 3 December 2016. He is currently working as a Real Estate Agent and pursuing his credentials to be a Real Estate Broker. God has used Ben in a mighty way over the last several years and I am confident that Ben will continue serving The Lord in his daily walk.

Stephanie Elese Blanton was born on 3 September 1985. I tagged her "Pretty Girl" immediately because she was and is so pretty! She is also pretty inside with a loving and caring heart which makes her the perfect nurse, which is her chosen profession. Stephanie is very gregarious and outgoing; she has multiple friends and is respected by her peers. Stephanie married Patrick Barnes on 10 December 2011. They reside in their first home as owners in Sugar Hill, Georgia. Patrick is a dentist and has started his first practice in Orthodontics in the Gwinnett County Area of Georgia. Stephanie is working part time at Northeast Georgia Hospital, Braselton, Georgia. Stephanie and Patrick officially welcomed Jackson Ross Barnes into the world on 2 June 2017. He weighed 7 pounds, 15 ounces and was 22 inches long! At this writing "Jack Jack" is two years old and growing like a weed!

So as we say in the ARMY, BLUF (Bottom Line Up Front), none of this would be possible without Gerann being by my side all these years. God has richly blessed our lives together so it is fitting that this book be dedicated to Gerann Elese Blanton!

CONTENTS

PROLOGUE

My father, Forrest Anderson Blanton, and my father-in-law, Jesse Thomas Smith, were both members of "The Greatest Generation". They served in the U.S. Navy during World War II in the Pacific Theater. Like most veterans of WWII neither of them ever shared much detail about their experiences both during the war or even stories of their "growing up" years.

With that in mind and knowing that my generation had their own story to tell, I set out to write this book with the purpose in mind to share my Vietnam War experiences with my children, grandchildren, extended family, and friends. My intention was just to get "my story" recorded so that primarily my family would know something of what their "Pop" did when he served his nation in uniform.

I had kept a daily calendar while in Vietnam and for a couple of years before and after as well. That calendar was the basis of most of the stories included in the book regarding Vietnam and some of the training leading up to my deployment.

Rather than limit "my story" to just Vietnam I decided to treat the book as sort of an autobiography. Thus, I began with some of my early recollections of growing up in Atlanta, Georgia. For most of the material recounting my early childhood, elementary school, high school, and college years, I depended on my memory, such as it is!

My intention was simply to get "my story" on paper. Publishing is something that I have only recently thought about. I never envisioned selling this book but as I stated, my sole purpose was to provide my family with something they could have to remember their "Pop" by.

The one thing I want my readers to understand about the Vietnam War is this; we (U.S. Military) did not lose the Vietnam War! All U.S. Military Forces were withdrawn from Vietnam in late March of 1973 in accordance with the peace agreement that was negotiated with North Vietnam. When Saigon fell and the NVA (North Vietnamese Army) overran South Vietnam, the U.S. Military only had a few U.S. Marines at the embassy in Saigon.

All that said, what follows is "my story" which I've entitled "Flying Low"!

FOREWORD — DAVID BAILEY

I have known Steve Blanton for well over 50 years. We've been friends and gone through many trials and tribulations together as college students and as United States Army Officers.

Steve comes from a hard working blue collar family. His family did not have much in the way of material goods but the love for family and country was over the top! In other words, Steve comes from good stock. Steve's parents were hardworking, patriotic, and most important, was the unconditional love they had for all. To be invited to Steve's house was always good. His family made you feel loved and welcome anytime you were there.

When I met Steve in 1966, we were freshmen (FROGS) at North Georgia College or NGC (now the University of North Georgia) in Dahlonega, Georgia. NGC is the military college of Georgia and FROGS are considered the lowest possible level in the Corps of Cadets. We managed to make it through FROG week reasonably unscathed. Steve and I had the usual ups and downs as Cadets at North Georgia. We played sports and did a lot of other things you do as a college student at a military school. We did manage to graduate in the normal four years!

Upon graduation, Steve and I were commissioned as Second Lieutenants in the U.S. Army. My father who was an active duty Army

Colonel at that time administered the oath of office to both Steve and me in the Commandant of Cadet's Office. What a thrill that was for both of us! My father told me later he was honored to do it and proud of both of us.

Steve and I went on Active duty on the same day. He went to Fort Eustis, Virginia for the Transportation Officer Basic Course (TOBC) and I went to Fort Gordon, Georgia for the Signal Officer Basic Course (SOBC). We kept in touch and several months later I caught up with Steve and his wife Gerann at Fort Wolters, Texas. Steve was attending Rotary Wing Flight School. I was on my way to Fort Huachuca, Arizona for my first duty assignment as a new Lieutenant. We all had a great time for about a week. We went to the Officers Club and played Bingo where Steve won a set of golf clubs and took up golf for the first time! I met several of Steve's flight classmates; we ate some great food and enjoyed fellowshipping with one another.

Several months later I received orders to Vietnam. Steve was about half way through flight school at Fort Rucker, Alabama where he was in Advanced Rotary Wing Training. Shortly thereafter he graduated and transitioned to Cobras (Gunships) and then onto Fort Eustis, Virginia for Aircraft Maintenance Officer Course (AMOC). When he finished AMOC he got orders for Vietnam. Steve got in touch with me and let me know that he'd be arriving in country on 21 August of 1972. As fate would have it, my job in Vietnam had me at Ton Son Knut Airbase in Saigon where Steve would be in-processed at Camp Alpha. He called me at my office shortly after arriving at 1200 hours on 21 August. Steve stayed with me in my downtown apartment until 29 August (his birthday!) when I took him to 8th Aerial Port at the airbase to catch a ride on a Huey that left at 0800 hours. Steve was assigned to the 18th Corps Aviation Company (CAC) in the Mekong Delta south of my location about 75 miles.

As the S-4 (supply and services) in my unit, I had Special Security

Detachments all over the Southeast Asia Theater. One was in Can Tho where Steve was assigned to the 18th CAC. I spent a good deal of time with the Supply and Services Detachments (SSDs) that were located in Vietnam. As it turned out the detachment in Can Tho needed a lot of assistance dealing with local supply issues. Steve and I got together as often as we could manage. Steve also was able to come to Saigon a couple of times as well. He and I saw former NGC classmates and other people we knew from previous assignments in the U.S. Army. These chance meetings turned into mini reunions and we enjoyed seeing everyone.

After Vietnam, Steve and I were both reassigned stateside. Steve went to Fort Eustis, Virginia and I went to Fort Bragg, North Carolina. We kept in touch and visited as often as our schedules allowed. I remember one occasion when Steve and Tom Arnold flew from Eustis to Bragg in a Huey. I met them at the airfield. When they started rolling their golf clubs across the tarmac concealed with duffle bags, I though the controllers in the tower were going to fall down laughing. I'll admit I was laughing pretty hard myself. We had a great day, played a round of golf, cooked steaks at my apartment, and then they flew back that night. We kept in touch and visited as often as our schedules allowed.

Steve got off active duty in August of 1974 and moved to Rutledge, Georgia to begin his civilian career as a teacher and coach. I got off active duty in 1977 and moved to Florida to begin my career in the corporate world. During the ensuing years, we both had families but continued to stay in touch.

We both returned to the Army; I in the U.S. Army Reserve and Steve in the Georgia Army National Guard. We continued to serve until retirement. Steve retired in 2008 and I retired in 1998.

Steve has continued to be actively involved in his church, Gideons International, community activities, and family. Our friendship includes two other NGC graduates. Randell Cline is from Bowling

Green, Kentucky by way of Grundy, Virginia. John Broderick is from Wilmington Island (Savannah), Georgia. The four of us have been good friends since NGC days. We have two golf outings every year. The good thing about golf is it's a sport you can play no matter how old you are! The foursome of Randell Cline, John Broderick, Steve Blanton, and David Bailey is a truly formidable group. In fact, we have won first place in the Ty Reed Golf Classic (a Charity Tournament that Steve puts on annually). What a great time we have when we all are together.

In closing, Steve has been a great friend and confidant to me as well as many others. He would give you the shirt off his back if you needed it. This book is truly a blessing and a testament to my close friend of many years. Enjoy!

FOREWORD — TIM REED

My name is Tim Reed. I remember well over forty years ago my wife Caren and the author's wife Gerann met and became friends in the small town of Rutledge, Georgia. Through their friendship, I met Gerann's husband, Steven E. Blanton. For some reason, that day I knew we would become good friends.

In a very short period after we met, Steve became my best friend. We played golf together (and still do), coached high school football together, and traveled together with our families every year on summer vacations. Our wives taught school together. Our children became best friends as well. I guess you could say we were one big family.

I will give you an example of our closeness but first let me share a pretty humorous story. Not long after becoming friends, Steve called one night to tell me that a bat had flown down the chimney into his house. He asked if I would come over to help. So, I grabbed my broom and headed over. When I arrived he was outside waiting. With both of us armed with our weapons, Steve turns to me and asked how I thought we should handle this situation. Holding my broom tightly I looked him straight in the eye and said, "Let's just go in and take care of business." Steve asked, "Are you ready?" I answered, "I think so." He asked again, "Are you ready?" Again, I said, "I think so." He asked a third time, "Are you ready?" I answered, "Go ahead, I'm right behind you." We laugh about that even today. Joking aside, Steve and I have always been behind each other since.

Let me give you a more serious example. In the spring of 1993, our oldest son Ty was tragically killed in an automobile accident in front of our home. He was 18 years old, graduating from high school, accepted to college, and ready to begin a new chapter in his life. By that summer, it became evident we could not stay in the same home. We loved the memories of Ty growing up in this home but it became quite unbearable having to see the site of the accident day after day. We searched and found a house in another small town about 10 miles away. In just a few months, my friend Steve, my best friend, sold his home, bought a house and moved his family just a few houses from where we live today. Now that's what I call a best friend.

Over the years, Steve has been asked to speak at many functions. Whether speaking to a church full of veterans on Veterans Day or to a graduating class at high school, or to just a few men at a prayer breakfast, you will always find his stories funny, others warm and thought provoking, and some touching on life's sorrows. Whatever the subject or occasion, you will see and hear that he is gifted at spotlighting faith and hope in every situation.

Steve is a great storyteller and speaker in person, so I'm sure this book will inspire as you read. However, Steve will be the first to tell you that it's not about him. It's about the reality of God in our lives.

What an honor to write this foreword for my dear friend Steve Blanton. I have not only been inspired by his book but am daily inspired by his life as not only a professional but more important as a Christian man in all he says and does.

As you turn the pages, prepare to laugh or perhaps shed a tear. More importantly, know that through every chapter is a reminder that as we all go through life, God is with us, comforting us, sharing all our joys and sorrows, but most of all loving us through it all.

I. GROWING UP

AND ELEMENTARY SCHOOL

I was in the backyard playing as little boys would do, and wishing that I had someone to play with. Suddenly he appeared out of the woods behind the 'outhouse' (fancy folks called it a privy but we were just ordinary folks). "Hey, who are you?" "My name is Steve, Steve Blanton, I live here, who are you?" "My name is Chris Walker; I live through the woods next to Ligerfelts Store". Chris had dark skin, like a permanent sun tan, and jet black hair. I was about five or six years old; I had not started school yet. I wouldn't start until the first grade, when I'd be six years old on August 29, 1954. Mother didn't want her "baby" to attend kindergarten. It was a new program and besides, "five years old is too young for school".

That was the start of a friendship that would last a lifetime even though Chris would meet a tragic early end to his life here on earth at the tender age of just 22. Chris lived in a huge two story house on Hollywood Road. His Dad, Lorre Walker, was a sign painter. They had a huge shop out back where Mr. Walker did his sign painting, two cement ponds where Chris and I sometimes went wading and a greenhouse on the hill next to the woods. We had some great times Chris and I growing up together.

1

Chris' Dad, Lorre, and his Mom, Glenis, owned a cabin at the foot of Sharp Top Mountain near Jasper in the North Georgia Mountains. It was a 'real log cabin', one large room with a fireplace, a kitchen built on to the back and a screened 'sleeping porch' all the way down the left side. There was a fresh spring running out of the mountain and Mr. Walker built a spring house on his place where they 'drew' fresh water. They also owned a 'campsite' near the Army Ranger Camp out from Dahlonega, Georgia, the home of North Georgia College (NGC).

I made many trips with Chris and his family both to Jasper and Dahlonega. We would climb Sharp Top and swim in Lake Grandview when at the cabin. Trips to the campsite near Dahlonega consisted of romping and playing in the thick woods, wading in the cold mountain streams, and sometimes fishing for at least 30 minutes until we got bored. We had to travel through Dahlonega in order to reach the Walker's campsite. I marveled at the site of NGC and the cadets walking upright in their sharp military uniforms. Little did I know, years later, I would be one of those cadets.

My two older brothers, Cecil and Robert, both joined the Marine Corps in the early fifties right after the end of the Korean War. This was exciting for me and further sparked my interest in the military. Cecil and Robert had finished 'Boot Camp' and were both assigned to Camp Lejeune, South Carolina. They had both gotten married, Robert to his boyhood sweetheart Inez Gazaway (More about Robert's marriage to Inez later) and Cecil to Ellen Buice. Mother and I went to visit them at Camp Lejeune. We rode the bus because Mother didn't drive. Family housing for enlisted Marines without children consisted of nothing more than a small trailer with a bedroom on one end, kitchen & bath in the middle and a small living room on the other end. It was not as large as most small present day campers. I slept on a pallet on the floor but I had a ball! We spent several days there and I was mesmerized by all the Marines marching around in their uniforms and looking sharp. My brother Robert put together a uniform for me. He pieced together some discarded insignia, found a Marine Corps hat that would fit me and sewed some Marine Corps buttons on my shirt. I was in 'Hog Heaven' playing like I was a Marine and sneaking around the trailer park 'shooting the enemy'! Can you see a pattern developing here? I didn't realize it until years later but I was destined to pursue a career in the military. God was working things out for me and I didn't have a clue at the time.

About my brother Robert and his marriage to Inez; well, he came home on leave from Paris Island, South Carolina. While home, he and Inez decided to go ahead and get married. I think my sister Joan and her husband Clyde "stood up" for them at the Justice of The Peace. Of course, you can't go back to the Marines immediately after getting married so Robert just stayed home with his new bride Inez, in other words he went AWOL! In a week or so, the MPs (Military Police) came and got him, took him back to the base, and threw him in the Brig (Jail)! His company commander found out, went to the Colonel and pleaded, "Sir, I've got to have Blanton, he's my company clerk and we're behind on everything." The Colonel agreed to let PVT Blanton (he was "busted" from his former rank of Sergeant) "do his time" under the supervision of his company commander. A few weeks passed, Robert typed up a promotion order on himself, put it in with a stack of other papers the company commander needed to sign, took it in the "old man's office" (that's the term of endearment for the company commander) one day and shuffled each item hurriedly under the commander's nose for a quick signature. So, that's how my brother Robert got his stripes back! You might say he earned them a second time!

The other boys in the neighborhood and I were always looking for adventure, for something to do that was fun but not expensive. Sizemore Avenue, the street I lived on, was perpendicular to Alvin Drive below our house. Up the street in front of my Granny Blanton's house was the first high point on Sizemore; this was about 100 yards from Alvin Drive and probably some 50 feet higher in elevation from Alvin Drive. The curbs were very crude so it was very easy to remove a section wide enough so that we could drive a bicycle through the curb and up the embankment that was immediately across Alvin Drive at the end of Sizemore. The embankment acted as a natural ramp so that with the speed gained from our 100-yard run down Sizemore we would cross Alvin Drive, go up the embankment and become airborne! With enough speed and timing the top of the bank with an upward pull on the handle bars, it was possible to achieve a height of five to six feet off the ground, what a thrill! The only problem was that you needed a reliable person to stand watch at the bottom of Sizemore and "wave you off" if traffic was coming in either direction. Of course there was a point when you just had to go ahead, regardless of the traffic and just hope for the best!

One day I decided that I'd go further up Sizemore past the Grady's house. This was another 100 yards or so but it gave you the opportunity to gain more speed, even though there was a slight dip when you went through the hollow just before my Granny's house. I started peddling as hard and fast as I could and by the time I passed my house about 60 yards from the jump, I was moving at a speed of about 25 miles per hour. My lookout signaled all clear and I peddled all the much faster, across Alvin Drive, up the bank, airborne! I must have been at least seven or eight feet off the ground, I almost came "un-joined" from my bike but I held on. When I landed, the bike went into about three pieces and I went flying head over heels straight ahead without my bike! I got up slowly, dusted myself off, gathered the pieces of my bike and immediately claimed a new "world record" for jumping the bank!

One of my first leadership positions was Lieutenant of the School Safety Patrol when I was in the seventh grade at John Carey Elementary School. My good friend James Bobo was Captain. We had a great time wearing our patrol belts and badges.

Our primary objective was to assist all the students at the several crosswalks in the neighborhoods surrounding our school. In that day, you either walked to school or caught a ride with your parents or neighbors, there were no school buses. I was responsible for Hollywood Road between Lingerfelt's Store and the curve just past Chris Walker's house. I would arrive early each morning, roll the metal 'silhouetted policeman' into the middle of the street on each end of my sector and then stop traffic to allow the students to cross safely. Each afternoon this would be repeated for the return trip home.

Every spring thousands of School Safety Patrols from all over the country would assemble in Washington D.C. for a huge convention. Several of us at John Carey were planning to attend the convention. The cost was forty dollars which was a great deal of money in 1961. I knew my parents could not afford to send me on that trip so I had resolved myself to the fact that I probably wouldn't be going. Well, I heard that a free trip would be awarded to one student based on citizenship and academics. Maybe there's hope yet, I thought! The selection came down to two students, James Bobo and me. James was awarded the free trip and I went home that afternoon sorely disappointed. Mother said, "Don't worry, we'll figure out a way for you to go." Somehow, someway they did and I had the greatest time of my life on that trip.

Regarding my family, we were poor but in many ways we had more than many in our neighborhood. During my early years, we had no electricity and we never had an "indoor bathroom". We had to go out back to the little brown building to do "our business". We had to carry water from my Granny Blanton's house until we finally got "running water" when I was about twelve years old.

My father, Forrest Anderson Blanton, was a simple man. He was a World War II Veteran (Navy) and for most of his working career he was a Union Painter. He had two speeds; wide open and stop! Once when he was in his fifties the foreman put a new man with my Daddy to "break him in". He was a young man, in his early twenties, and at the end of the day he begged the foreman to put him with someone else because my Daddy was "killing him" with the pace he worked.

My Mother was the disciplinarian. She administered the punishment when I got "out of line". She would send me to cut my own switch; once I came back with the tiniest little switch you could imagine. Well, after Mother cut her own switch, considerably bigger than mine, that cured me from choosing a switch that was too small! Mother was raised on a farm in South Georgia and she knew the value of a dollar. She controlled the purse strings in our family; we didn't have a great deal but we always had plenty to eat, new clothes when we needed them, and a warm house.

My oldest brother Cecil was always proud of his service in the United States Marine Corps. He always bragged on me and in his own way was one of my encouragers.

Robert and Inez moved to Oklahoma in the late 60s and reared their family in the Oklahoma City area. He was a long-distance trucker for about 40 years (more about that later). He was always a positive influence on my life and oftentimes he would stop over to visit us when he had a trip that brought him close by.

My Sister Joan has always been a source of strength. She helped Mother and Daddy tremendously, especially in their later years. Joan is and has always been special to our immediate family and our children. My brother-in-law Clyde and I became close during all the years that we sold peaches together during the 70s and early 80s. I told folks that I sold peaches in the summer so I could afford to teach school! We spent many days together and I learned a great deal from him regarding dealing with people and conducting business.

My brother Harold was nine years older than me but in many ways

I assumed the role of his older brother, particularly after I left home for college. Harold was never able to really grow up; I believe he was misdiagnosed as a youth. His problem, I believe, was socially maladjustment more than anything else. We lost him to heart disease at age 57. I really miss him. Through all his troubles, he really had a good sense of humor and loved his family; he was one of my best cheerleaders.

I need to mention my nephews and nieces. Since I was the 'baby' in my family, I became an Uncle at the ripe old age of six! My sister Joan and her husband Clyde had two boys. Jeff was the first of my nephews and nieces so he made me an Uncle. Jeff used to tell all his friends at John Carey Elementary School that I was his big brother. Jeff is a builder and remodeler. His brother Perry quickly became known as Peeps and still is even to this day. Perry lives in Texas with his family and has the knack of being a superb salesman, just like his Father Clyde.

My oldest brother Cecil and his wife Ellen had five children, Angie, Eric, Tim, Dennis, and Cecil Jr. Angie was a sweet little girl and is a lovely lady. She is a devout Christian who truly "walks The Walk". Eric has always worked hard to provide for his family. He has persevered through a number of difficult circumstances during his life. Tim served his country proudly in the U.S. Army as a Ranger and did a combat jump during the liberation of Granada during the early 80s. Dennis owns a flooring company and is a skilled professional. He is a meticulous craftsman and his work is beyond compare. Cecil Jr. is a fine Christian man who loves his family and works hard to provide for them. He has overcome many setbacks in his life and I'm proud to call him my nephew.

As I alluded to earlier, my brother Robert and his wife Inez moved their family to Oklahoma in the late 60s when Robert drove for Transcon Trucking Company. Their oldest son Bob was struck with Polio as a young boy. Even though he has struggled at times with his physical limitations, Bob has a strong will and has managed to work and provide for his family through the years. Randell served his country as a member of the U.S. Army and the 82d Airborne! He suffered some life-threatening injuries as a young man after his military service. He has stepped in after the death of his father and has assumed the role of protector and caretaker for his Mother. Robyn was the 'baby' in her family. As a young girl growing up she was always positive and loving. She has been the primary provider for her family and has been a source of strength and encouragement to her parents. Sadly, we lost Robyn to brain cancer on 23 May 2019.

Now back to the Washington trip. The train ride to Washington was exciting. It seemed to take forever, because we stopped in every little town along the way to take on new passengers and let others off. Other than riding the Nancy Hanks from Atlanta to Macon once, I had never been on a passenger train.

We toured all the monuments, Mount Vernon, and the Washington Zoo. There was a gigantic parade and I was so proud to march wearing my Safety Belt and Lieutenant Badge. I ran all the way to the top of the Washington Monument and stood in awe of the gigantic statue of Abe Lincoln sitting in that big chair. I was most impressed with the changing of the guard at the Tomb of the Unknown Soldier and with the Iwo Jima U.S. Marine Corps War Memorial. I was beginning to gravitate toward a career in the military and I didn't even realize it at the time.

After returning home I started to prepare myself to attend West Fulton High School. The city of Atlanta Schools in those days had grades 1-7 in Elementary School and grades 8-12 in High School. I was excited and somewhat apprehensive at the same time. After all, there's a huge difference between a 13-year old and a 17 or 18-year old. Nonetheless, I couldn't wait to start my high school career as a West Fulton Owl!

2. WEST FULTON

The next fall I was off to West Fulton High School in Atlanta, Georgia. Elementary School was grades first through seventh. High School was grades eight through twelve. Eighth graders were sub-freshmen, now that's as low as it gets in high school! What's lower than a freshman? A sub-freshman, that's what!

I was impressed with the Cadets in the Junior Reserve Officer Training Corps (JROTC). Eighth and ninth graders were not eligible to participate in JROTC; I couldn't wait until my sophomore year so I could wear those uniforms and march around the parade field.

My eighth-grade year was fairly uneventful. I enjoyed being in high school but I was somewhat overwhelmed with the enormity of the whole situation. West Fulton High School was huge, three floors and a basement with a "cracker box" style gym. The venerable old building looked very majestic with huge white columns in front and sitting high on a hill overlooking Bankhead Highway. There was a practice football field in the back with concrete stands on the far side and a crude quarter mile track. The school had about 1200 students; a big change from John Carey Elementary with its approximately 300 students. Additionally, as I mentioned I was a sub-freshman which meant that everybody else had a higher status than me and my classmates. Nevertheless, I was in high school! I enjoyed going to several football games with my friend James Bobo. Our team wasn't very good but the atmosphere of the games was always exciting. I remember going to the old Ponce De Leon Ballpark (the minor league Atlanta Crackers played there) for a couple of games. All in all, I'd say that I had a pretty good first year in high school.

Then came the ninth-grade year; a couple of key events occurred during this my second year in high school. We had all heard the talk during the summer about federal forced integration. This had been brewing since 1957 when President Eisenhower sent Federal Troops to Little Rock, Arkansas to oversee the integration of the public schools there. Sure enough, the first day of school at West Fulton and there they were. The sum total of two Negroes (this was the accepted term in that day rather than the derogatory slang of "nigger"). Now I don't even remember their sex, maybe one boy and one girl. It was much to do about nothing. We'd see our buddies between classes and ask, "You seen one?" "Naw; you?" It was more of a novelty than anything else. Little did we know what was coming in two years?

Mrs. Wyndelts was a gray-haired lady, very homely looking and not very attractive (that's about as nice as I can be). James Bobo and I had her for Algebra. Now I was pretty good at adding, subtracting, multiplying, and dividing numbers. But when they asked me to do that with letters of the alphabet, well, I got real confused! Mid-term grades came out and James and I both were failing! We had to do something really fast. "Let's go talk to her," I said. "OK, we'll go to her room before school tomorrow," said James. We showed up early the next morning and Mrs. Wyndelts seemed sincere in wanting to help us. She offered to tutor us each morning before school for 30 minutes. The rest of that semester, my sister, Joan, would drop us off early on her way to work. James and I faithfully showed up each morning for our extra tutoring session. Our hard work really paid off. Best I can remember we rose our grade about 10 points each but it still added up to a big fat "F"! That was the first class either of us had ever failed. Unfortunately, it wouldn't be the last one for me.

I couldn't wait for spring that year. I had always been a pretty fast runner as a boy growing up in my neighborhood on the "hill". I could usually outrun most of the other boys. When I was thirteen I joined the Explorer Scouts. One of the annual events was something called the "Exploreree". This was a weekend campout with various events. I entered the 50-yard dash, 600-yard run, standing broad jump, and sit-ups. I came away with three first place ribbons and one second (this was in the 50-yard dash; the boy who beat me jumped the gun but they didn't call a false start). I was most proud of my accomplishment in the sit-up event. This was not a timed event; each boy did sit-ups as long as he could and as many as he could. Most of the other competitors had already given out after 50 to 100 completed sit-ups. I started my count already behind the other boy by about 100 (he had started before me). These were straight leg (no bent knee) sit-ups with a partner holding your feet and counting. I passed the other boy at around 400; he was slowing considerably and I was doing about two for each one he did. Finally, he quit at 600 (quite a feat). I knew I was ahead on the count but did not realize the number I was at. I dropped my hands and quit, though I could have done more. "Nine hundred eighty-five (985)", exclaimed my counter. I immediately said, "I wish you'd have told me my count, I'd have done at least 15 more for an even 1000!"

Now, fast forward back to spring of my ninth-grade year; I decided that I would put my natural talent to good use and "go out" for the track team. I was intrigued with the hurdle event so I decided to try out for the Intermediate Hurdles (they were just 36 inches high as opposed to 39 inches for the high school). I ran track for two years at West Fulton but I wouldn't discover my real natural talent for running until I moved to South Cobb High School in Mableton, Georgia, at the beginning of my Junior year (more about that later).

Summers seemed much longer back then. I have fond memories of playing football in the vacant lot across the street with my buddies, James and Danny Bobo, Howard Buice, and several others. Adrian Wheeler was a couple of years younger but we had to let him play because it was his vacant lot. I remember on the most amazing things that happened one summer was the excitement when we learned that we would be getting street lights in our neighborhood! Every kid on my street was sitting under the street light that first night waiting for it to come on. We let out a big cheer when it finally flickered on and dimly lit a small portion of our street in front of my house.

During my growing up years one of my summer jobs was picking blackberries. I would go up and down the old car track along the creek next to Hollywood Road and fill my bucket with huge, juicy blackberries. The old car track as we referred to it was the abandoned rail line of the street cars; the city of Atlanta had retired all the street cars in favor of electric trolleys sometime in the mid-fifties. I would get a rounded up gallon of blackberries in a little while and off I'd go in my neighborhood to sell my goods. First, I'd go home and skim enough off the top for Mother to make a delicious cobbler. The going price was $1.25 for a whole gallon; I'd usually sell them after calling on just a couple of the neighbors. One summer, I saved nearly $20 selling my blackberries!

Miss Georgia Dairies was my first official job after my freshman year. My birthday is August 29. I wasn't going to be fifteen until almost the end of the summer. Back then you could not get a Social Security Number until age fifteen. I really wanted the job so I fibbed about my age! It worked out because as soon as I received my Social Security Number I turned it in to my employer. I was a "soda jerk", working behind the counter making ice cream sundaes, spinning wheels (milk shakes), and scooping delicious Miss Georgia Ice Cream into cones and cups. I was making a huge salary, 52 cents an hour! When school started, I had to quit my job because I couldn't work on school nights.

I filled in when I could on weekends and holidays. This continued through my sophomore year leading up to my junior year. After another long summer, I was ready for my sophomore year of high school!

September 1963, time for my sophomore year! First day of school and they were everywhere! Instead of two, we now had fifteen Negroes in "our school"! Well, after a few days things settled down and it really wasn't a big deal at all. Really, fifteen in a school of 1200 was just barely noticeable. We had no idea what was coming the next year.

I was now a sophomore and eligible to sign up for JROTC. When I came home with my uniforms I was really excited and couldn't wait to wear it on our designated dress days.

After a few weeks, it was announced that we would be having a best dressed competition on uniform day. Well, I was determined to win that competition; I worked for a couple of hours "spit shinning" my shoes until you could see your face in the toes. Mother carefully pressed my pants, shirt, and jacket (we couldn't afford to send them to the cleaners). The day of the competition arrived and I was all dressed and ready; my sister Joan was at the street blowing her horn. As I was leaving, Mother said, "Wait; take this". She handed me a clean, pressed and folded white handkerchief. "Mother, I don't need this!" "Take it, put it in your back left pocket and button the pocket," she said. I reluctantly did as she said, thinking the whole time that she didn't know much about military matters.

After a careful inspection, I was chosen from my platoon to go up for the best dressed competition. There were about twenty of us in two ranks of ten each. The Cadet Colonel and his staff "eyeballed" us head to toe and one by one he'd say, "OK, you can go back to your platoon." Finally, the competition came down to one other first year cadet and me. It was a virtual tie so they began asking questions from the FM 22-5 (the official drill manual). I had studied well, and I knew all the answers, but so did the other cadet. Finally, one of the staff officers said, "Well, I suppose we'll just have a tie." Then it happened, the Cadet Colonel said, "Do either of you have a clean, pressed, and folded white handkerchief in your back pocket?" I started grinning like a "mule eatin' briars"! "Yes Sir, I do!" I was so proud when I came home wearing my best dressed cord around my shoulder. I learned a valuable lesson that day. Mother apparently did know something about military matters.

I had some mild success running Intermediate hurdles on the "B" Team. The "B" Team was composed primarily of 9th and 10th graders. I placed second and third in some meets. However, I wasn't completely satisfied; I didn't feel that I was reaching my full potential. Back in my neighborhood, I could run and play all day without getting the least bit winded; I remembered the success I had enjoyed a year or so earlier at the "Exploreree". Maybe, I'll try distance running next year, I thought. But next year at West Fulton didn't come for me and many others.

One of the most valuable skills I ever learned was in my sophomore year when I took a typing class. Mrs. McGruder ("Granny Gruder") was our teacher. She would stand in front of the room and drill us over and over until we learned the keyboard. I amazed myself with the quick progress that I made with both speed and accuracy. At the end of the semester I was typing between fifty and sixty words a minute with only one or two errors. Throughout my career, the keyboarding skills I learned from "Granny Gruder" have served me well.

During the summer break, I worked with my cousin Jerry Petty, who was a brick mason, as a laborer for Doug Waugh Construction. I was the "Mud Man"; back then we mixed the mortar in a large tub with a hoe. It was back-breaking work but I managed just fine, even though I was only about 148 pounds soaking wet! I would usually come home tired and filthy; I would rig up a shower outside with the water hose and lather up in front of the entire neighborhood. Of course, I wore my swim suit.

Another huge milestone was that I had turned 16 years old just prior to the start of school and I now had my very first driver's license. I wanted a car really bad. My brother-in-law, Clyde, told me that Mr. Day over on Mack Drive had an old car he wanted to sell. Daddy took me over to take a look at it; a blue 1948 Plymouth, 4-door, flathead six engine with "suicide doors" (the rear doors opened backwards). The interior was rough but it ran like a sewing machine and the paint was practically new. Mother and Daddy loaned me the $150.00 that Mr. Day was asking and suddenly I was now a car owner. I paid Mother and Daddy back $10 a week until the debt was settled. I don't know to this day where they got the $150.00 but at the time I wasn't concerned with that. First chance I got, I made a trip to Sears & Roebuck in West End where I had a new set of seat covers put on front and back for $20 bucks. Then I saved my money and had all four door panels recovered in leatherette at a local upholstery shop on Bankhead Highway. I put a shine on the old Plymouth with Turtle Wax and I was set!

During the next couple of years, I had some great times in that ole Plymouth. A couple of trips stand out in my memory. Chris Walker, Howard Buice, Steve Sprayberry, and I took a weekend trip to the Walker cabin in Jasper. We went swimming in Lake Grand View, rode the mountain roads, and visited every eating joint in Jasper; there were about three or four as I recall. Eventually we got bored. We heard about a square dance on Saturday night in Ellijay, just a few miles north of Jasper. We headed out, sure that we would meet some girls. Somewhere along the way we managed to purchase some sure 'nuff authentic North Georgia Moon Shine! Needless to say, we did not pick up any girls and to this very day I don't know how we got back to the cabin. We woke up the next morning with bloodshot eyes and aching heads. Once again, The Lord was looking out for me.

First day of school, junior year, I'm driving my very own set of wheels. I was on top of the world; what could go wrong? There seemed to be a lot of activity in front of the school, folks carrying signs, police cars, just a whole lot of commotion. It didn't take long to find out what was going on. Thanks to bussing and federal mandates, West Fulton High School was now fully integrated, 50% White and 50% Negro! By the end of that first week, West Fulton was 90% Negro. Most of the White students left for other schools, including me. Some went to O'Keefe High School next to Georgia Tech (not sure why they weren't being forced to integrate since they were in the city of Atlanta) while others went to live with relatives in other counties where schools were still segregated. It was a sad beginning to my junor year of high school. I'll never forget the senior girls who were helping with typing the transfers; they all were fighting back tears because their school was being ripped apart.

My parents decided that it would be best if I moved in with my brother Robert and his family. They lived in Mableton, Georgia, which was in the school district for South Cobb High School.

3. SOUTH COBB

I moved in with my brother Robert and his family in Mableton, Georgia and registered at South Cobb High School (SCHS) in Austell, Georgia.

Larry Fenley was about my height, blond hair with an easy-going manner about him. "I heard you're a hurdler," Larry said. "Yeah, I ran Intermediates at West Fulton," I said. Larry was an excellent hurdler, one of the best in Cobb County and Region 5AAA (the largest classification in the Georgia High School Association, GHSA, at that time). So, Larry Fenley and I became best friends through a common interest, running. He lived in Powder Springs, a few miles up Clay Road from South Cobb High. Over the next several years through high school and college, I would spend a lot of time with Larry and often would sleep over at his house.

In 1964-65, my first year at SCHS, we had one of the top basketball teams in the State of Georgia. I wanted to play basketball but my skills just weren't up to par with that of the SCHS team so I quickly dismissed the idea. Instead, I'd concentrate on improving my skill as a hurdler by learning from Larry, whose skill level was close to where I wanted to be. I did enjoy attending many basketball games. The Varsity Boy's Coach was Wayne Dubose, a tall quiet man with a flat top haircut. He also coached the Varsity Cross Country Team (more on that later). Our basketball team lost just five games the entire season. They lost all five to Osborne High School, twice in the regular season, once in the Cobb County Tournament, once in the Region 5AAA Tournament and once in the State Tournament. The largest margin of victory was five points in one game. Ken Brewer and Mike Bracewell were great high school basketball players on the SCHS team. My good friend Howard Buice, had moved to Smyrna and was a student at Osborne High School, often reminded me of those five games. By the way, Osborne High School won the State Tournament that year. They had a fantastic player named Mike Norholdtz.

I decided that I would go out for the football team. Because I had missed all the summer pre-season practice I was relegated to playing on the "B" Team. This was primarily tenth graders and a few juniors. I was the first string center for the team; we played a limited schedule, just seven or eight games. We had a great year, undefeated, won six and tied two as I recall. All in all, this was a good experience and because I had "sacrificed" and helped out the "B" Team, many of my teammates assured me I'd have the inside track to being first string varsity during my senior year (more on that later).

Larry Fenley and I had started working out with several other boys getting ready for the Track and Field Season. Ted Missildine was the Track Coach; he also coached on the varsity football team. I thought to myself, if I do well during track season then I'll be points ahead come football season!

I improved tremendously during the season in the high hurdles. Larry's technique was much better than mine so I learned a great deal from him. I improved in the 120-yard high hurdles from the mid 18s to about 16.5 by the end of the season. Though Larry was consistently in the mid to high 15s, by the end of the year I managed to qualify for the finals of the high hurdles in the Cobb County Track Meet. Larry and I both were in the final race of six runners. Larry was third as I recall but I came in last, which was still good enough for a point. Even though I had improved quite a bit, I decided that hurdling was not my forte; I'd have to find another event to excel at during my senior season next year.

Larry had been talking to me about going out for Cross Country. I enjoyed running and since I'd had earlier success with at least middle distance events in the Explorer Scouts, I decided to give it a go. In fact, I had briefly gone out for Cross Country at West Fulton during my 9th grade year, only to have that cut short because of some problems with my kidneys. As I recall, the doctor said I had some enlargement of at least one kidney and he recommended that I quit running.

Wayne Dubose was the cross country coach; this was like an extra duty for him since his primary job was the boy's basketball coach. Coach Dubose was a tall quite man with an easy going manner about him; he was a perfect fit for our cross country team. We had been running since track season; coach came up with the idea of a 500-mile club. To be a member was pretty simple, you had to run 500 miles. We had a big chart in the dressing room and each day we'd log our miles. Once you reached 500, you received a medal signifying that you were a member of the 500-mile club. This was a very clever strategy because it established a great training base and we actually got into a sort of competition to see who would be the first to 500 miles and then the second and so on.

I quickly became one of the leading runners on the team; in fact, I was the number one runner. George Caldwell and Dewy McKown were next and then Terry Graham. Larry Fenley was our 5th runner.

In cross country, the first five runners score; you get one point for first, two for second, three for third and so on; the low score won. Every course was different but the distance was always two miles back then (nowadays high school cross country is usually 5K or 3.1 miles). We won most of our meets and were heavy favorites to win the 5AAA

Region Cross Country Championship. My best time was 10:30 (ten minutes, thirty seconds) and I was really looking forward to the Region Meet. It was held at the Atlanta City Water Works off Howell Mill Road. The course was two laps around a lake with a couple of big hills to negotiate. Well, I had one of my worst races of the year. I finished 3rd behind George and Terry. Dewy was fourth and our team won handily. Our first four places blew everybody away. Larry came in around 20th place so we won going away. Coach Dubose was so proud of us that day and we were all excited to take the first place trophy back to South Cobb! We had a great season but I felt that I had not performed my best at the Region Meet. I would make amends later that year during track season.

After cross country season, several of us continued to run and log miles so we would be ready for track season. Larry Fenley ran with us even though he was not a distance runner. Our group consisted of George Caldwell and Terry Graham, both juniors, Dewy McKown and Thomas Price, both sophomores, Larry Andrews, a freshman, Fenley and me, both seniors.

We had a great track season. One of the highlights was a trip to the University of Florida early in the season, March I believe, to run in the Florida Relays. This was a college meet but as a recruiting tool, a number of high schools were invited. We had a great time, stayed at the Marriott in Gainesville, Florida. Coach entered me in the Invitational Mile Run, seventy-two runners crowding the start line for position. I got boxed in early in the race and finished about top one fourth in 4:48, my best time to date. We won most of our dual meets and were one of the favorites to win the Region Meet which was held at Westminster High School, a private school in the "well to do" section of North Side Atlanta.

Before I get to that, another interesting thing happened during my senior year. As spring approached, a lot of the boys were talking about who they were going to take to the Junior-Senior Prom. I never planned to go, I wasn't really even dating at the time and since I had transferred from West Fulton the year before I knew very few of the girls at South Cobb.

One day after English Class, my teacher, Ms. Joan Landes, asked me who I was taking to the prom. Well, I told her that I wasn't planning to go. She was incredulous! "I can't believe you're not going to the prom during *your* senior year," she practically screamed! So, she said without warning, "Why don't you take me?" Ms. Landes was single, just a few years older than me, maybe mid-twenties, and a nice looking lady. What could I say? I said OK. That didn't last very long; apparently the principal, W.G. Stephens, got wind of it and put the brakes on those plans.

I eventually did go to the prom. Marion Pinnell, a good friend of my brother Robert and my former Explorer Scoutmaster arranged a date for me with the daughter of one his other friends. Martha, I don't remember her last name, was an attractive girl but very shy and withdrawn. She attended Sylvan High School in Southwest Atlanta. To say that my Senior Prom was boring would be an understatement. I never saw or heard from Martha again after that uneventful night.

Now, back to the Region 5AAA Track Meet; I was feeling very good and in top shape, peaking at just the right time. I felt my best chance was in the Mile Run. I was also entered in the 880 Yard Run (half mile) and the Mile Relay (each runner ran one lap and handed the baton to the next runner). I had run a decent 880 during the season, in fact I had broken the school record with my best time of 2:03.5 but I felt that the mile was my best distance.

Most of the talk concerning the mile was about a runner from Marietta High School named Mathias, don't remember his first name. About fifteen minutes before the mile run, a huge rain storm came through and soaked the track which was the old-fashioned cinder type.

To say the least, it left the track a muddy mess. I lined up at the starting line with about 25 other runners, two from each school in the Region. We were staggered until the first turn; I started in about the third lane. At the sound of the gun, we were off. I broke clean out of the first turn in about fourth place and settled in on the backstretch at a brisk pace. First lap was 1:03 for the leader and 1:06 for me, a little fast. I moved up to third on the second lap, Mathias was leading by about ten yards over the second runner who was just in front of me; the rain started again more vigorous than earlier, it was pelting me in the face, I could hardly see more than twenty yards to the front. Second lap was 2:18 for Mathias, I was at 2:20 just a few strides behind but still in third. The pace slowed somewhat during the third lap, Mathias was at 3:30, still leading and I was at 3:33 still in third but now more than 10 yards behind Mathias. I made my move coming out of the turn onto the backstretch. I passed the second-place runner easily but Mathias was still a good seven to eight yards ahead. Going into the final turn, I made my move and closed to within no more than two good strides behind first place. The rain was still coming down almost sideways now. Coming out of the last turn I could see Mathias beginning to falter somewhat. I knew I had to go now, just 50 yards from the finish line I summoned everything I had left and began a furious kick. I moved to the outside and pulled even with Mathias just 20 yards from the finish line. With one final push I eased past him and came to the finish line a good five yards ahead. My time was 4:39.9, a new personal record for me. I had run the last lap in 66.9... I was the Region 5AAA Mile Champion!

Larry Fenley was the first to congratulate me, then George Caldwell who finished in fourth place as I recall. Then the whole team came over and congratulated me along with Coach Missildine. It was a great feeling and definitely the high point of my high school track career. I would continue running for many years to come, through my college days at North Georgia and on into my adult life.

I qualified for State as the Region 5AAA Champion; Larry Fenley also qualified in both the 180 yard low hurdles and the 120-yard high hurdles. Larry had a best of 20.4 in the lows and 14.4 in the highs. Well, just to "cut to the chase", we both got a serious case of "senioritis" after the Region Meet. We didn't train very hard and consequently neither of us did very well at the State Meet which was held at Grady High School in Atlanta, Georgia.

Graduation was fast approaching. Most of my classmates were talking about where they were going to college. Fenley had been offered a running scholarship to attend the University of Georgia in Athens. We were about four weeks from graduation day and I didn't have any college plans. Coach Missildine told me that I should continue my running career; he thought I had the potential to really excel. He arranged an interview and visit to LaGrange College; he knew the track coach and recommended me.

Mother and Daddy took me down to LaGrange on a Sunday that spring. The campus was small but very neat, a typical small college setting. The LaGrange coach, I don't remember his name, offered me a partial scholarship and an "assistanceship". If accepted, I'd be working in the athletic department part time to earn part of my tuition. LaGrange College was a private institution and very expensive. Even with the financial aid, I knew we couldn't afford it on Daddy's salary. He was a union painter and made good money but he didn't always have steady work. Besides all that, it just didn't feel right; I came to realize later in life that even though I wasn't saved at the time, the Holy Spirit was speaking to me and working things out for my life.

I thought what should I do? I started to think about North Georgia College (NGC) and all those times I marveled at the uniformed cadets walking about on the campus in Dahlonega. I really can't explain it but I was being drawn to North Georgia College. After a few days, I decided to just go ahead and fill out an application to NGC. About two weeks later, a letter arrived addressed to me. "Congratulations, you have been approved for enrollment with the freshman class at North Georgia College beginning with the fall quarter in September 1966."

4. NORTH GEORGIA COLLEGE

I was getting excited about the prospect of going away to college. A couple of weeks before I was to leave, K Mart opened their first store in Atlanta, Georgia. Jayne Mansfield was the special guest at the grand opening; I managed to get close enough to catch a glimpse of her. Man was I disappointed, she looked like a store mannequin with make-up caked so thick that when she smiled it appeared that her face might break!

My brother Robert had registered for a door prize during the grand opening. He was notified by phone that he had won a Shelby GT-350 Mustang for a weekend! It was gorgeous, jet black, trimmed in gold with raised letter tires. Robert told me that since this was my last weekend before heading off to NGC that I could borrow the Mustang; he was going on the road for a trucking trip and wouldn't be able to use it. I slid in under the wheel, put the key in the ignition, turned it, and the engine immediately came to life, what an awesome sound I thought. I pulled out of Robert's driveway, slowly cruised down Magnolia Drive and onto Alabama Road. I eased my foot down on the accelerator and the power was unbelievable! The speed limit was 55 and I was at 60 before I could say Mustang! This was going to be a really cool weekend, and I already had a date for Saturday Night.

I don't even remember the girl's name but we had a great time riding around in the coolest car I'd ever seen. We went to the drive-in movie on Fulton Industrial Boulevard. I wanted to go there so I wouldn't have to get out of the car! Every head in the place turned our way when we pulled in. Later that night we cruised into the Varsity in downtown Atlanta near the Georgia Tech Campus. Again, all eyes were on us as we rumbled into the parking lot and parked in the upper deck. I left the motor running and then revved it up before shutting it off.

After I took my date home, I met James and Danny Bobo. We drove out to I-75 North in Cobb County. Several miles of the interstate highway were finished but not opened to the public yet. James got out of the Mustang and moved the sawhorse that marked the beginning of the new highway; I eased past and then James replaced the sawhorse. From a standing start, we reached 100 mph in a matter of seconds! When the speed odometer read 135 mph I began to realize that this is probably not a good idea so I started to decelerate. In retrospect, this was just one of many times that The Lord was with me and looking out for my well-being, because I certainly was not looking out for myself!

Mother and Daddy took me to Dahlonega in early September for Orientation Week. I remember Mother writing the check for my first quarter; $319.00! Wow, that was the most money I had ever seen written in a check.

I learned later that Orientation Week was unofficially referred to as "Frog Week", a time when the upper-class cadre (the Cadet Officers and Cadet NCOs) spent a week "whipping" the new freshmen into military shape.

Most of the freshmen had family and friends with them. After all the goodbyes were said and parents, etc. were gone it started. "Frog drop and give me 10 push-ups, now!" For the next week, we marched, ran, did push-ups, and generally were harassed during every waking hour. After the initial shock, I decided that they wouldn't break me. I would survive and come through in good shape. When it came to the running, the cadre and my fellow freshmen classmates couldn't keep up with me. I could run all day, especially at the ridiculously slow pace that was double time. We learned to spit shine our shoes (I had an advantage here from my JROTC days at West Fulton High), arrange our foot lockers in accordance with (IAW) the Blue Book, make our bunks with military corners, arrange our closet with each hanger exactly two fingers apart and generally keep our area "squared away" at all times.

After Frog Week, the upper classmen eased up somewhat because now we had to start our classes. Man, was I in for a real shock. It didn't take me long to realize that I should have studied more in high school and played less.

Every Wednesday afternoon we would have a 'dust inspection' and military events such as close order drill, etc. On Saturday morning, we'd have academic classes (the ones we missed on Wednesday afternoon). Fortunately, freshman year was the last time this program was in effect. We still had inspections, drills, etc. but they scheduled them on Saturdays for the most part.

Another event during freshman year was mandatory Church attendance. On Sunday mornings, we were required to dress in our uniforms and leave campus to attend the Church of our choice. I tried the Catholic, Methodist, and Baptist at different times. However, sad to say, my church was often the local pool hall downtown. Some of my buddies, Randell Cline, Benny Cleveland, David (Beetle) Bailey, and I would 'attend Church' while playing a little eight ball or rotation!

I will never forget my first day in College Algebra. I was terrified just thinking about my bad experience at West Fulton in Mrs. Wyndelts Algebra Class. Mr. Leffingwell wrote an Algebraic Equation on the left-hand side of the chalk board. The chalk board extended from the left wall all the way across the front of the classroom to the door. He took a piece of chalk that was about four inches long and began working the equation and talking with every step. After about three minutes, he placed an equal sign near the door and put the answer next to it. He turned and said, "What are your questions?" I knew I was in trouble!

I had barely passed the required placement test as an incoming freshman in Math but I failed the English placement test. I was in "Wild Bill" Roberts History Class, more about him later. My first quarter grades were C in English, D in History and F in Algebra! Because the English Class was a remedial course, I did not receive credit for it so my Grade Point Average (GPA) after the first quarter was 0.5! This was a huge hole that I spent the next four years gradually crawling out of.

Larry Fenley was at the University of Georgia (UGA) on a track scholarship and doing better than average academically. Larry was very bright and even though he studied very little, he managed to do well. I decided that I had to get out of NGC and make a fresh start at UGA so I applied about halfway through my first quarter. Once my grades were final for the fall quarter, UGA sent me one of those letters that started off something like this: "We appreciate your interest in the University Of Georgia but…" Needless to say, I was not accepted to UGA so I resolved myself to staying at NGC and trying to make the best of my situation.

I soon met Herbie Height who was also into running distance. Herbie was short, maybe 5'6" at best. We decided to train together and we set as our goal to unseat Larry Duncan as the champion of the three-mile Crown Mountain run. The mountain run was the final event during a two-day series of events in the spring that included track and field along with other special events such as team tug-of-war. Larry Duncan had won the mountain run during the previous two years and now as a junior everyone was already penciling in his name as the winner for the third year in a row.

Herbie was a natural and was a dedicated runner whose self-discipline was to be admired. We would train hard Monday through Thursday. Most weekends, I would slack off; oftentimes I would "hitch-hike" to Athens and spend the weekend with Larry. We'd go to dances and usually buy a quart of Black Label or Bud. I should have stayed at NGC and studied my books and continued my running. I would start back on Monday training with Herbie and by Thursday I would be almost back up to speed with him. This was a cycle that I repeated all too often.

The day of the Crown Mountain Run had arrived. Herbie and I were confident, but so was Larry Duncan. The course started in front of the Chow Hall next to the Drill Field, down the side road onto Highway 60 next to the Smith House, right turn and then up a steep incline to the turn off the highway, another right turn onto a brief flat area of about 200 yards before ascending the final half mile up about a 30 degree hill to the fire tower on top of Crown Mountain. It was about 1.8 miles from the start to the top of the mountain. From there descending quickly and curving around the mountain where it flattened out somewhat before winding through the cemetery, then through the gate between Sanford and Lewis Halls, around the Drill Field road to the left, past the Science building and then to the finish line. The course measured three miles, 1.8 uphill and the final 1.2 downhill, a grueling course.

The gun sounded and we were off. Quickly Herbie, Larry Duncan, and I separated from the rest of the field. By the time we reached the turn off Highway 60, Herbie had established about a 10 yard lead followed by Duncan and then me in third about five yards behind Duncan. I passed Duncan about half-way up the half mile 30-degree hill and was now in second place about eight yards behind Herbie. By the time I reached the top of the mountain at the fire tower, Herbie was a good 15 to 20 yards ahead. You see while I was still trudging along to reach the top, Herbie was accelerating about twice my speed going downhill. I could never recover. I lost sight of Herbie going through the curves and the cemetery; I knew I couldn't catch him so I just concentrated on holding off Duncan for second place. Herbie finished in the low 16s and I came in at 16:15 well ahead of Duncan whose time was about 16:45. We had accomplished our goal; Larry Duncan was no longer "King of Crown Mountain"! I had mixed emotions, knowing that I really had not done my best. I knew that my slackness in training and my poor discipline had resulted in my second-place finish. I immediately began to think about next year and how I would win the Crown Mountain Run.

SUMMER BREAK 1967

Summer break flew by; I worked at Continental Can Company's corrugated container plant in Atlanta. Larry Fenley's Dad, Lonnie, was a foreman there and he got Larry and me both on the night shift. Larry worked on the line as the palletize machine operator. As the finished boxes rolled down the line from four different directions, they would pass through the palletize machine to have metal bands placed around them, two on each side. It sounds simple but the pallets came quickly and staying ahead was absolutely essential because if the pallets of boxes backed up, then the printing/cutting machines would have to shut down and a stopped machine means lost production. Lost production means lost money! Larry was very efficient at operating the palletize machine; in fact, he usually kept up to the point that oftentimes he was standing around waiting on the boxes. Consequently, management thought he was goofing off since he was standing around, visiting other workers, etc. On the other hand, Larry's cousin Doug was the palletize operator during the day shift and he was continually behind. Management would look out from their "Ivory Tower" and see Doug working feverishly to try and keep up. They would smile and say, "Wow, that boy Doug is a fine worker!" You see, it all has to do with perception.

I worked on the corrugator. This was the machine that made all the cardboard. The corrugator was about 100 yards long. All the raw materials would be feed in at the start and through several processes of crinkling for the middles, cutting and gluing the finished sheets of cardboard would come out the other end. That's where my job was, a "catcher" of the finished product. We worked with a partner because many times the sheets of cardboard would come out as large as 8' x 12' with two or three thicknesses. A stack of 20-25 sheets would weigh upwards of a couple of hundred pounds. We would stand up the stack between us, push from each end to straighten out the stack and then lift and place it on wooden floats to be pushed away once they were stacked as high as we could reach. The smaller sheets were no bargain either. They would come extremely fast and we would work individually, one on each side of the conveyor alternating taking every other stack. The corrugator never shut down; it operated 24/7. The only time we got a break was when the machine broke down and required maintenance. I was not a Christian then but I often found myself praying that the machine would break! We worked 12 hour shifts, 4PM to 4AM. It was a little strange; we'd clock in and there would be these other folks clocking out. Then 12 hours later we'd clock out and those same folks we saw earlier would be clocking in. It seemed that nobody ever left the plant!

My brother Robert owned a boat and I would go with him and his family often to Lake Allatoona. We would swim, ski, and go on long boat rides. Sometimes we'd set trot lines, usually in the coves. These consisted of several milk jugs tied together with baited hooks at various depths hanging from each jug. We would set the trot lines at night and next morning we'd go back and if we were lucky then we'd just pull up our fish, usually catfish. I always thought it was sort of like a lazy man's way to fish.

One weekend Robert had a road trip. He was a truck driver so he was gone a lot. I convinced him to let me borrow the boat and take it to the lake by myself. Larry and I headed out to the lake, just the two of us, pulling my brother's 14 foot Sears & Roebuck red and white boat powered by a 40 horse Elgin outboard motor. I felt so proud and so grown; I was almost 19 years old! We had a great time; we took turns skiing and went on a long ride up to the dam.

We had a great time with no problems except for a couple of things. The lake was up quite a bit from recent rains. On my last turn to ski (I was doing slalom, one ski) I was feeling pretty confident. My last pass through the cove I swung really wide, almost even with the boat. Since the water was up you could not distinguish where the shoreline was. Before I realized what was happening, I had gone up onto the bank in water that was no deeper than six inches! Before I could change my direction, the water ran out and I was on the grass; my rear fin of the ski dug into the ground and I came out of the ski! I was moving pretty fast, probably about 20 mph, and I was propelled through the air! Fortunately, I had the presence of mind to turn loose of the ski rope. I turned about two forward somersaults and landed on my rear sitting straight up! I was young and wiry so other than being embarrassed and shook up I was alright.

We loaded the boat and were getting ready to leave. We had dressed and secured everything in the boat; I reached for my wallet and it was gone! Larry and I combed the entire area and all along the shore line, no luck. I didn't tell my parents or Robert about the lost wallet. A couple of weeks later, my mother received a phone call from a man who said that he had found my wallet washed up on the shoreline. I was off for the weekend; Larry and I had gone fishing at the "Wilderness Camp" on Lake Allatoona. Of course my Mother thought the worse, that I had drowned! There were no cell phones back then so she had no way to get in touch with me. I called home that evening; Mother was so happy that I was OK she didn't fuss too much about the lost wallet, whew!

SOPHOMORE YEAR:
SEPTEMBER 1967–MAY 1968

Fall quarter was just a few weeks away; I received a letter from the Commandant at NGC informing me that I had been selected to be a member of the cadre as a squad leader in Golf Company. Apparently, I had been recommended by one of the upper classmen and even though my GPA as a freshman was miserable, they thought I had some leadership potential. I was excited!

Second squad, fourth platoon, Golf Company was my squad. Joe Childs, freshman, Chuck Clarkson, slick sleeve (PVT, no rank) sophomore, M. L. Miller, freshman and Kelly Bonnette, slick sleeve sophomore were the members of my squad.

During Frog Week only the freshman were there so all the squads were rebalanced with the slick sleeve upper classmen the next week before the start of classes. I really got into the spirit of Frog Week; it was definitely more fun being on the giving end rather than the receiving end. In addition to all the running, push-ups, and general harassment, we also taught the new "Frogs" drill and ceremony from FM (Field Manual) 22-5. I thoroughly enjoyed participating in Frog Week; this would be the first of three that I was privileged to be a part of. I sort of dreaded the start of classes but I knew I had to improve academically or I would be out before winter quarter.

I had not declared an academic major. Probably at least half the rising sophomore class had already decided. My idea was that someday I wanted to be a high school coach so Physical Education made all the sense in the world to me. We were known as "Jock Majors" and were subjected to much ridicule from many of our classmates. Granted we probably had an easier road than majors in Chemistry, Biology, or Math but it was no picnic, especially when it came to certain required classes that we had to take out of the department. All Physical Education majors had to declare an academic concentration. I decided on Psychology; I figured that way I had the mind and body both covered!

Under classmen were not allowed to have automobiles. This was a privilege reserved for seniors only. I had bought a 1954 Chevrolet Bel Air from my brother Robert for $150.00 with some of the money I had earned during the summer. It was four doors, six cylinders (Chevy didn't come out with V8s until 1955); crème colored and ran smooth as a sewing machine. After a few weeks, I decided that I would bring my "ride" back to Dahlonega. One of the "dirty feet" (this was the slang we used for local commuter students) had told me about a lady across town who would allow me to park my car at her house. This arrangement worked perfectly for a while. One Friday I had packed my duffel for a trip home. I made the approximate one mile walk to pick-up my car when I realized that I had forgotten my shaving kit. I didn't want to walk back and get it; that would take too long and delay my leaving for home. I decided to take a chance so I drove through the back gate next to Dairy Queen, up the hill to Sirmans Hall and parked in the back of the building out of sight. I quickly ran up to my room, retrieved the shaving kit, back down, into the car, and off for my weekend. I arrived back on campus Sunday evening around 1830 (6:30PM) after walking from my hiding place. I had been in my room no more than 10 minutes when the CQ (charge of quarters) knocked on my door and informed me that the Company Commander, Cadet Captain Roberts, wanted

34

to see me in his room. Apparently, the Battalion Commander, Cadet LTC Fort, had seen me on Friday when I parked behind the dorm. His suite overlooked the parking lot and he just happened to be in his room. It took me several afternoons walking the quadrangle to work off all those demerits! I was more careful from then on regarding my car.

In February of 1968, the *Rec Clubs* (this was the fraternities for the female students who resided in Lewis Hall) planned a *Twerp Dance*. This was a version of the *Sadie Hawkins Dance* where the girl asks the boy for a date. I had dated Faye Cato a couple of times. She was a nice enough girl but I could tell that there really wasn't much attraction in the relationship from either of us. I was in Biology Class with Tom Owensby and his girlfriend, Deanna Lloyd, was a roommate to Gerann Smith. I really didn't know Gerann but I had definitely noticed her lately. Oh yea, she was in my Biology Class, in fact I believe that we were actually lab partners when we dissected frogs! Unbeknownst to me at the time, Faye had her eye on Jim Crupi so she suggested to Gerann that she (Gerann) should ask me to the dance and she (Faye) would ask Jim. As it turned out, I had planned to go home that weekend so I said no. Afterwards I thought, you dummy, you just blew your chance! After some reflection, I came to my senses and called her back and told her that my plans had changed and that I could go. That started our courtship which lasted the last two and a half years of college. We were married June 6, 1970 and will celebrate our 49th Anniversary during 2019. (More on this in Chapter 5)

During Winter Quarter a bunch of us were sitting around on a Friday Afternoon with the prospect of a long weekend three day without anything to do (It was either Washington or Lincoln's Birthday; I don't remember which). Somebody said let's go on a road trip! So David Bailey (Beetle), Bob Bowers, Merril "Otto" Osterhout, Tom Hancock, and I climbed into my 1954 four door Chevy Bel Air and tore out for Washington, D.C. Beetle's Dad, COL Jack Bailey, was stationed at the Pentagon and his parents had a home in Arlington, Virginia. We pooled our money and managed to buy gas along the way (gas prices were 30-35 cents per gallon). We probably consumed more beer along the way than my Chevy consumed gas. That's just another example of The Lord looking out for me in those days!

We drove a little over 600 miles in about 10 hours and we certainly didn't have Interstate the entire route back then. Beetle called his Mom along the way so she was waiting up for us when we arrived early Saturday morning before daylight. We didn't really do much while we were there. Beetle's Dad gave us a tour of the Pentagon; the enormity of the building and what it stood for was overpowering. We left out for Dahlonega on Monday morning. Now this was in the middle of February in Washington D.C.; it was below freezing and had been for several days. We didn't get out of the city and my old Chevy boiled over, running hot as a fireball. My antifreeze was inadequate for the frigid temperatures of Northern Virginia. Beetle's Dad came to our rescue; he paid the service bill for us and we made it back to Dahlonega safe and sound.

When Spring Quarter started, I had improved my GPA but it was still around 1.5; it would take another year to crawl out of the hole I had made for myself during my first year of college.

Herbie Height had transferred so when I started training for the annual Crown Mountain Run, I was on my own. I worked hard, put in many miles, and mixed in some interval training. The buzz was again focused on Larry Duncan who was now a senior. Both Herbie and I had beaten him the year before, but many folks said that Duncan had a bad day or he wasn't feeling good, etc.

The gun sounded and I was off quickly in almost a dead sprint. I knew that I needed to separate early so that I wouldn't get caught up in a bottle neck going up Highway 60 before the turn-off. I settled in about five yards behind Duncan who was leading. The two of us opened up a good 20 yards on the rest of the field as we turned off Highway 60. I knew I had to make my move before we started the severe incline up to the fire tower. I measured Duncan and summoned a quick burst of speed and blew by him on the flat area leading up to the initial climb. I opened up about five yards by the time we were one third up the hill. I leaned into the mountain so that my knees were almost touching my chest with each stride; my lead was a good 10 yards when I reached the pinnacle. Immediately I began to accelerate, taking off the brakes and racing down at a feverish pace. If I can be out of sight when Duncan reaches the top then he'll quit, I thought. Before going into the first turn about 30 yards below the pinnacle, I stole a quick glance over my right shoulder. I thought I saw him but I couldn't be sure; my best bet was to race as if he were on my heels.

When I reached the cemetery, I looked back quickly but I couldn't distinguish weather I was seeing tombstones or Duncan! I exited the cemetery, turned right into the gate between Sanford and Lewis Halls, then to the left onto the perimeter road around the drill field. I was about 200 yards from the finish line and then I heard a few of the crowd yelling, "Go Duncan, go!" Oh no! He has closed the gap I thought as I looked back one final time to see him at least 100 yards to my rear. I coasted to victory! I was King of Crown Mountain! This would be the first of three in a row but perhaps the most satisfying one. Bob Stein, a freshman, was third. Two years later we would be partners in the most famous run in North Georgia College history. My time was slower than the previous year, about 16:45, but I didn't care, I had won!

SUMMER BREAK 1968

My old Chevy was getting tired; I needed a better car for my final two years in college. I was working at Continental Can Company with Larry Fenley and making decent money. Minimum wage was $1.60 per hour; we were making about $2.65 per hour! My parents went with me to Nalley Chevrolet in Buckhead. I looked at several cars but a sweet looking 1966 Mercury Comet, two-door hardtop, caught my eye. It was solid white with blue interior (leatherette), 3 speeds on the column with a 289 cubic inch V8 engine and only two years old with low mileage. I don't remember the price but my parents co-signed with me to get the loan through GMAC (General Motors finance Acceptance Corporation). I was set! First thing I did was to go out and buy some big speakers and woofers and an 8-track tape deck. The speakers were small compared to the behemoths they're putting in some cars today. I spent an afternoon at Marty Welch's house in Southwest Atlanta and he installed everything for me. Man, it sounded really good with my Johnny Rivers tape turned up high!

Gerann and I took a couple of courses at Georgia State College in downtown Atlanta during the summer. She lived with her Aunt Kathryn and Uncle Melvin near Maddox Park and I would go by and pick her up each day in my slick Mercury. Unfortunately, I spent too much time playing during the summer and not enough time in the books so I made a 'C' and a 'D'. Only the 'C' would transfer but at least I added five hours credit toward my graduation goal.

JUNIOR YEAR: 1968–1969

I was selected to be in the *Cadre* as a Platoon Sergeant in Golf Company. The Platoon Leader was Bob Slaughter, a really good man. Bob made one of our golf trips a few years ago. Several of our old NGC friends get together each fall for a golf outing on Clark Hill Reservoir. Beetle's sister Margaret and brother-in-law Dr. Dan McAvoy own a lake house and they graciously allow us to use it as our hideaway for that week each year.

Frog week was great! I really got into it more so than the previous year. I was in great shape so I ran the Freshmen Frogs until their tongues were hanging out!

Soon classes began and it was down to work. I began to get into my major which was Physical Education. One of the first classes in our major was *Fundamentals and Principals of Physical Education*. I still have the book; it weighed about two pounds and was about 500 pages! The first day of class Coach U. G. (Ulysses Grant) Matherly, Department Head, gave us our indoctrination. "Gym is a boy's name, Phys Ed is a soda, PE is something you do in the Restroom; you are Physical Education Majors!" You didn't dare use any of the slang terms normally associated with Physical Education around Coach Matherly or you would receive a severe reprimand and tongue lashing. He did, however, instill in each of us a certain pride in our chosen field of study.

One of the required out of department courses was *Anatomy and Physiology (A&P)*. This was normally taken during your junior year as a PE, Oops, I mean Physical Education Major! *A & P* was taught by Ben Sanders ('Uncle Ben') in the Biology Department. I took the class during winter quarter along with Randell Cline, Grant Matherly, Jr. (Coach Matherly's Son), Charlotte Daniel, and Ronnie Mitchell. The first day of class Uncle Ben announced, "Are there any PE Majors in the class?" Each of us "Jocks" raised our hands barely above shoulder level; we knew that we would be 'marked' from that point forward. The class certainly lived up to its reputation and Uncle Ben did nothing to dispel the stories about how tough he was. We learned the human body from head to toe, all the muscles, bones, nervous system, lymphatic system, circulatory system, respiratory system, digestive system, etc. I really studied more than I ever had for any other course; I was never more proud of a 'D' in my whole life! I had survived *A & P!*

Dahlonega was not exactly a party town. There was a Dairy Queen (DQ) across from campus at the foot of Crown Mountain and a Taste

Tee Freeze on the other end of town. We had an ancient movie theater, a pool room, and the Dixie Café near the arch to the main entrance of campus. So, we were always looking for other places to go in order to have a good time. One such place was Helen, Georgia and the Chattahoochee Inn and Restaurant (The Hooch). The primary reason the Hooch appealed to us was the cold beer on draft; they didn't check IDs! Their food was OK too. In the four years at NGC, I made numerous trips to the Hooch with several different groups and it's only by the grace of The Lord that we always made it back to Dahlonega in one piece!

Much of our time in Military Science Classes during our junior year was designed to prepare us for ROTC Advanced Camp at Fort Bragg, North Carolina. Our subjects included small unit tactics (platoon and company level primarily), basic soldier skills, and military organization with emphasis on the importance of something called 'Commander's Intent'. Our military, unlike that of any other in the world, operates as a cohesive unit with the primary purpose to achieve the intent of the Commander. This enables every leader within the chain of command to make decisions independent of direct supervision so long as that decision moves the unit toward the ultimate accomplishment of the mission (Commander's Intent).

Spring Quarter was fast approaching and I began to prepare for my defense as King of Crown Mountain. I increased my mileage and mixed in some variable speed training as well. Larry Duncan had graduated the year before and there really wasn't anyone being touted as capable of unseating me. Nonetheless, I stepped up my training and when race day arrived I felt ready. As it turned out, by the time I turned off Highway 60 to begin the assent up the mountain, I was pretty much by myself. When I reached the top of the mountain, Bob Stein was about 15 yards behind me. By the time Bob reached the top, I was a good 30 yards or more ahead and out of site. I cruised to victory. I don't remember my time but I think it was around 17:00, my slowest yet but still good enough to win.

SUMMER 1969

This would be a summer to remember. I had arranged to ride the train to Arlington, Virginia and then ride to Fort Bragg with David Bailey (Beetle). Fort Bragg is one of the hottest places on Earth during the summer months. We reported in on Sunday, 15 June 1969 and the camp ran for six weeks to Sunday, 27 July 1969.

There were thousands of ROTC Cadets from all over the country there. This was one of the absolute requirements before you could be commissioned as a Second Lieutenant in the US Army. Everybody took it seriously. Most of our training centered on jungle warfare since we were still heavily involved in the Vietnam War. We had classes on camouflage, cover and concealment, escape and evasion, and small unit tactics with emphasis on platoon and company sized units.

We stayed in two story WWII vintage barracks. They were made primarily of wood, had old plumbing, and outdated electrical wiring. There was no air conditioning so we usually slept on top of the covers with windows open, begging for even the slightest breeze.

My bunk mate (beds were stacked two high, I had the top bunk) was Ray Barbee. Ray was from Clemson University. It didn't take me long to figure out that Ray was way behind when it came to military matters. We quickly formed a close friendship and I made a point to help Ray with everything I could. I taught him to make his bunk with military corners, spit shine his boots, tuck his uniform properly with the 'gig' line straight, and I worked with him regarding drill and ceremonies in the FM 22-5. We usually sat together during classes and I helped him every step of the way.

They kept points on each of us and at the end of camp the top cadet in each platoon would go on to competition at the company level, then battalion level, then brigade level and then overall top cadet at camp. I thought I probably had a decent shot at getting the top spot in my platoon. I had scored over 90% on all our written exams, had received an outstanding rating when in different leadership positions, including a turn at Company Commander and had received superior ratings on all inspections, both individual and barracks. I finished number two in the platoon. Ray Barbee finished first! I didn't regret anything I had done; I knew that I had given it my best shot. This may have been my first indication that maybe I had some talent to be a teacher?

On 20 July 1969, I was sitting in the Officer's Club at Fort Bragg watching on TV as one of the most memorable events in the history of mankind unfolded. Neil Armstrong took the first steps onto the moon as he uttered the famous words, "This is one small step for man, one giant leap for mankind". To this day, I marvel at what we were able to accomplish in the space program. The excitement of the "Space Race" against the Soviet Union was something that most Americans followed closely and the fact that we beat them to the moon was a point of pride for everybody.

SENIOR YEAR:
SEPTEMBER 1969 — MAY 1970

After a successful Advance Camp at Fort Bragg, I was hopeful that I might get one of the company commands for my Senior Year at NGC. It was not to be; I received a letter in August informing me that I had been selected as a Platoon Leader in Golf Company. I would finish my career at NGC having been in Golf Company all four years, not a bad thing at all.

I was First Platoon Leader; Jim Crissey was the Golf Company Commander. Frog week was fun as usual but I was anxious to get on with my Senior Year and graduate in the spring with my degree and commission as a Second Lieutenant in the U.S. Army.

The year before, I had signed a contract with the U.S. Army and began receiving a whopping fifty dollars a month as an advanced ROTC Student! I also worked in the Chow Hall during my last two years. In addition to those two sources of income, I hired on my senior year with Johnny Stone at the Pizza Palace. I made pizzas and ran deliveries to the campus of NGC. There was no dining room so we did a great delivery business, especially on the weekends when there was a dance on campus. Each delivery was worth twenty-five cents! On each run I may have as many as ten or twelve deliveries on my back seat and in the trunk of my '66 Mercury Comet. It was not uncommon to rack in twenty or more dollars in deliveries on a good night; that was big cash in 1969-70 dollars! I also stocked groceries one night a week at a small local grocery store.

Needless to say, I didn't have much time for studying but fortunately I was into my major and minor subjects during my last year and the subjects came fairly easy. My grades weren't honor roll by any means, but solid Bs with an occasional A or C. By the time I graduated, my GPA had risen from a low of .5 (that's point five!) during my freshman year to 2.34 at the end of my senior year; certainly not cum laude material but I was proud of the improvement.

At this point I must give Gerann her due. After we started dating during winter quarter of my sophomore year, my GPA started a steady climb upwards. In fact, I've said many times that if I hadn't met Gerann I would still be in *World Literature Class* at NGC!

Scabbard and Blade was a small select military honor society on campus that had a long history of being a well-respected organization that strived for excellence. In recent years, they had come under some scrutiny primarily because of some of the questionable initiation rituals they purportedly employed. Nevertheless, many still believed it was an organization worthy to aspire to. Each fall quarter the 'Blade' would *Tap* (invitation) a few selected Juniors and Seniors to join the organization. There was always much anticipation and discussion among the corps of cadets regarding who might get tapped. Because of my success at ROTC Advanced Camp, my name was being mentioned as one who may get *Tapped*. I had given this a lot of thought and was really undecided what I would do if indeed I was *Tapped*.

One night about 30 minutes after Taps (lights out), I heard footsteps in the hallway and the distinct sound of sabers rattling. The 'Blade' was on the prowl to *Tap* new members. Sure enough, there was a knock on my door. I said, "Come in." I don't remember who the cadet was but he walked over to my bunk (I was on top), laid his saber on my shoulder and said something like, "Steve Blanton, you have been deemed to be worthy of consideration for membership in the Honor Society of the Scabbard and Blade. If you accept this challenge then step out into the hallway." I had made my decision. As he was exiting my room, I said, "Close the door before you go." I rolled over and after considerable second guessing of my decision I went back to sleep. Eventually, the Scabbard and Blade was banned from the campus of NGC (after our graduation). I believe they've since been reinstated and perhaps they have changed some of their initiation rituals.

There were only two fraternities at NGC, REX and Sigma Theta. Neither was affiliated with a national fraternity. Each fall REX and Sigma Theta would have their version of '*Rush*' when they would invite a select few students to become members. I had several friends in each fraternity but I had not been invited to join either one during my first three years at NGC.

It was rare that a senior would receive an invitation to join REX or Sigma Theta. However, when the *Rush* started I was invited to join REX.

I never confirmed this but I believed that Tom Owensby, President of REX and boyfriend of Deanna Lloyd (they actually got married during our senior year), probably sponsored me. Since Deanna and Gerann were roommates, I figured that perhaps had an influence. I accepted and went through a week-long initiation ritual which included among other things being forced to take ice cold showers, drink entire bottles of A-1 steak sauce (to this day I don't use steak sauce!) and endure the rack for extended periods of time. This entailed placing your heels on the bottom bunk support bar and your elbows on the top one and hanging there until every muscle in your body began to quiver with cramps.

We had some good times at REX picnics and dances ('*Jukin*'). All in all, it was a good experience and it afforded me the opportunity to enlarge my circle of friends.

Another high point in my senior year was the ROTC Flight Training Program. This was a '*pilot program*' that was being implemented in selected ROTC Programs. Since NGC was one of only four colleges and universities with a Military College Rating (the others were Citadel, Texas A&M, and Virginia Military Institute), we were approved to have the program.

We received college credit for enrolling in the course that consisted of flight training, both ground school and flight time (40 hours) in a Cessna 150 and an opportunity to receive our private pilot's license at the end of the course.

My flight instructor was Horace Steele, a wily WWII pilot who flew *The Hump*. *The Hump* was the name given by Allied pilots in the Second World War to the eastern end of the Himalayan Mountains over which they flew military transport aircraft from India to China to resupply the Chinese war effort of Chiang Kai-shek and the units of the United States Army Air Forces based in China. Mr. Steele was strictly 'old school'; he flew 'by the seat of his pants' and exuded confidence.

I had about seven or eight hours flight time and I felt that I was getting close to that magical moment when I would solo. We had done a couple of touch and go's (that's when you land and immediately give full throttle, flaps up, mixture rich, and go into another take-off. Mr. Steele said, "After you land this time, taxi back to the end of the runway so we can do another takeoff from a standing start."

I came in just about right and stalled it onto the runway, came to a stop, turned around, and taxied back to the end and repositioned for another takeoff. I checked all my gauges, altimeter, flaps full up, clear right, clear left, clear overhead, full mixture rich, brakes off, full throttle; suddenly Mr. Steele pulled the throttle out and in a flash he was out of the airplane, standing on the ground! "What are you doing?" I said. "You don't need me anymore," Mr. Steele said as he grinned from ear to ear. "Give me two more touch and go landings," he said.

I thought; well here goes nothing. I shoved the mixture knob all the way in and gave it full throttle. I was off the ground quicker than normal without the extra weight of Mr. Steele on board. This is not bad I thought as I banked into a 90 degree turn left and leveled off at about 500 feet AGL (Above Ground Level). I turned another 90 degrees and started my downwind leg and then it hit me! I've got to land this thing without Mr. Steele next to me! I turned onto my crosswind leg and started a gradual decent then onto my final approach slowing my airspeed and 'milking' in flaps to get the aircraft in a slightly nose high attitude. Steady as she goes, here comes the runway, pull back on the stick, a little more flaps and then she just stalled onto the runway! Wow, I did it! Then flaps up, full throttle, mixture knob in, and I'm rolling toward another take-off. The second time around was easier than the first, I had soloed and would get my ROTC Wings the next day in class!

A few weeks later, I was out solo one afternoon in the local area. I found a nice open field which was ideal to set up for soft field landings.

I had done two practice approaches and figured I had just enough time to do one more. The procedure was to set up on final approach, 'milk' in full flaps, slow airspeed to about 40 knots by pulling the throttle out slowly, mixture knob full in, then at about 200 feet AGL (above ground level) you were to abort the landing by reversing the procedure i.e., flaps full up, mixture knob full in, throttle full in, and then start climb out to cruising altitude.

On my last approach, I raised the flaps full up, pushed the throttle full in, pulled back on the stick and pulled the mixture knob out! At about 300 feet AGL the engine started coughing, I was losing power! Suddenly the engine quit! I realized what I had done; by pulling the mixture knob out, I had cut off my fuel!

I didn't have enough altitude to restart the engine. I banked hard to my left performing a descending 360 degree turn while milking in full flaps, pulling back on the stick to slow my airspeed to 40 knots and finally stalling the airplane to a landing on someone's cow pasture! The field was anything but smooth and as I rolled to a stop, my head was banging on the roof of the cockpit.

After my heart rate slowed a bit, I exited the aircraft and began a visual inspection to insure we didn't have any damage. Everything looked okay so I climbed back in, restarted the engine, and was taxiing to get into position for a soft field take-off. About that time my radio blared, "Blanton what in the H____ are you doing?!" The other instructor, Donald Otter, happened to be flying over with another student and saw me in that cow pasture.

My response was that I had some engine trouble and had to land in order to check it out; everything was okay and now I was going to take-off. I didn't want to tell him that I had cut my own fuel off! Mr. Otter came back with, "You turn that engine off and wait right there; Mr. Steele will be there shortly!"

I figured I was in a heap of trouble. The old farmer that had been watching all this from his barn on one end of the field came over and did his best to encourage me. After all, I had landed in a space that was about half the length of the runway at Wimpy Field. I came in just over the top of the barn. There was a creek running perpendicular at the end of the field and I was standing on the brakes hoping I would be able to stop before putting the little Cessna 150 in the water!

Mr. Steele arrived about 30 minutes later. As he exited the truck and began walking toward me I started with my apology. "Mr. Steele I'm so sorry, I don't know what I was thinking; I was shooting practice approaches for a soft field landing and . . ." He interrupted me, "You pulled out the mixture knob, didn't you?" I sheepishly admitted that was exactly what I had done. He put his arm around me and said, "Don't worry about it, now you know that you can really do a soft field landing!" Ultimately, that stupid mistake boosted my confidence; I knew from that point forward that I could make an emergency landing if the need ever arose. Of course, my fellow classmates had a great deal of fun with me for several days.

Doc Waller was one of our best student pilots. He and Claude Grace were planning to fly in a four seat Cessna 172 from Dahlonega to Blairsville to pick up their dates for the Sweetheart Ball. This was in early February 1970. The weather was typical for North Georgia at the time of year, cold, overcast, and a chance of rain. Doc and Claude never made it to Blairsville. Their plane was found about four days later. Apparently the wings had iced over and they went straight into the ground. It was a very sad time at NGC.

One evening in early spring, maybe around mid-March, Bob Stein and I were jogging with Jim Crupi around campus. Bob and I had been increasing our running to get ready for the annual Crown Mountain Run in May. Jim was not an avid runner but he was just running to get in better shape. We were talking about several things as we jogged along. Jim asked how far we usually ran and we both said, "Oh, depending on how much time we have, maybe five or six miles." That got Jim to thinking, he said, "How far do you think you could run without stopping?" Without much thought I remarked, "We could probably run from Gainesville to Dahlonega."

Well, that's all Jim needed. He grabbed that idea and ran with it, figuratively speaking. He came up with the idea of the *'Gainesville-Dahlonega Memorial Run'* to be dedicated in honor of all the NGC cadets who had given their lives in Vietnam. When Jim came to Bob and me with his idea, I thought to myself, what have we gotten ourselves into? That's twenty-two and one half miles over mountains!

Bob and I began stepping up our training. We were both in pretty good shape but we weren't real sure that we could do 22.5 miles over mountain roads. Our test run came about two weeks away from the *Memorial Run*. We had Jim take us to the city limits of Gainesville. Our goal was to run about half way, which was Murrayville, Georgia, approximately 11 miles. A few days later, we did the second leg, Murrayville to Dahlonega, another 11miles or so. This leg was the toughest with the elevation steady rising. We knew that we were in for quite an undertaking.

Meanwhile Jim was busy promoting the *'Gainesville-Dahlonega Memorial Run'*. He invited Governor Lester Maddox, but he wasn't available. There were news releases on the Associated Press and United Press International wire services along with articles in the Atlanta Journal and Constitution Newspaper.

Jim wanted us to carry a torch throughout the run. We figured that would be too heavy and dangerous so we settled on carrying a mock torch made from lightweight aluminum. Scott Shemwell worked on the actual torch (with real flames!) that we would carry from the top of Crown Mountain onto the campus of NGC.

On 23 April 1970 at 4:15PM, Mayor Randolph Waters of Gainesville presented Bob and me the mock torch and we began our 22 ½ mile run. It was a hot day with clear skies. All along the route there were folks cheering us on.

We made the first leg to Murrayville with little trouble. The second more mountainous leg was much more difficult. When we were ascending Crown Mountain our time was at about three hours, 20 minutes. Just before we reached the apex of the mountain, I glanced over at Bob and he was beginning to wobble. He was very pale and I knew he was about to fall. There were people lining both sides of the road so Bob was quickly attended to and taken to the NGC Infirmary for further treatment.

Scott Shemwell handed me the lit torch and man was it heavy! To complicate matters, the fuel was leaking down the handle onto my arm. Scott struggled to keep up with me carrying a fire extinguisher in case I went up in flames! He dropped back when we came into view of the crowd that was gathered at Memorial Hall to greet us.

I was amazed! There were hundreds of students gathered, along with the Color Guard, Blue Ridge Rifles Drill Team, and the Band. As I was running down the mountain I kept thinking about Bob and hoped that he was okay.

The Mayor of Dahlonega, Fred Jones, and the President of NGC, Dr. Merritt E. Hoag, both were there to receive the torch. I was totally exhausted. This was back in the day when athletes didn't pay attention to hydration like they do now. Bob and I had run the total distance of 22 ½ miles over mountainous roads without taking in a single drop of water along the way. We were both suffering from dehydration. I have no doubt that's why Bob fell out and I wasn't in too great a shape either.

I mustered enough energy to stand at attention and salute while holding the lit torch high above my head with my left hand while the Band played the National Anthem. I presented the torch to Dr. Hoag, not sure exactly what I said, something like, "Please accept this torch in honor of all the North Georgia Cadets who have given their lives in service to our country in South Vietnam." Thankfully, Dr. Hoag kept his remarks brief and then dozens of folks wanted to shake my hand. I could see Gerann standing there with a tall glass of ice cold lemonade. Finally, I made my way to her and gulped the lemonade down so fast that it nearly came back up.

Several folks insisted that I go to the Infirmary and get checked out so reluctantly I did so. Once I started to hydrate I was fine. I will admit that I was a little sore the next day but after a couple of days I was back to 100%.

A couple of weeks after the *Memorial Run* the time had come for my final race on Crown Mountain. Having won the last two years, I was in line to do something that had never been accomplished before by winning the Crown Mountain Run three years in a row.

We were all at the starting line in front of the Chow Hall. Coach Matherly was giving the starting instructions when a freshman runner raised his hand to ask about the layout of the course. Coach Matherly began giving a lengthy description of the course when in mid-sentence he became flustered and he said, "Just follow Blanton!"

I was not aware of any serious challengers other than Bob Stein, but just in case, I planned to get out quick and put some distance between myself and the rest of the field before we reached the turn off Highway 60. Bob was definitely capable of beating me but I was determined to give it my best and hopefully hold off his challenge. With the sound of the gun we were off! I sprinted out briskly the first 100 yards and made my way down by the Smith House Restaurant and then right on Highway 60. By the time I reached the Dairy Queen, I had a good 20 yards on Bob. When I reached the top of Crown Mountain the nearest runner, Bob, was just beginning his climb up the steepest last 50 yards to the apex. I let the brakes off going down the mountain and breezed through the cemetery. When I came through the gate between Lewis Hall and Sanford Hall onto the campus I was the only runner in sight.

As I crossed the finish line next to the Chow Hall the second-place runner, Bob, was just entering the campus. King of Crown Mountain three years in a row!

We were just four weeks away from graduation! I couldn't believe it, I recalled four years earlier when I arrived in Dahlonega thinking that four years was a long time and now it was almost over.

Gerann had been busy planning our wedding. She had done her student teaching at Clarkesville High School during winter quarter. During spring quarter, she had her first teaching job at Lumpkin County High School in Dahlonega.

I had gotten my private pilot's License and actually had about four or five hours of flight time remaining on the 40 that the government had paid for. David Bailey agreed to go flying with me one afternoon. We took off from Wimpy Field near Dahlonega, flew to Gainesville where I did a couple of touch and go landings, and then headed back to Dahlonega. I decided to fly back over Lake Lanier to enjoy the beautiful scenery around the lake. 'Beetle' and I were talking and having a great time; I really wasn't too concerned with the map because it was a clear day. Visibility was virtually unlimited. I turned north and headed away from the lake toward Dahlonega. After a few minutes, we approached the town but I couldn't pick out Wimpy Field even though visibility was not a problem. I started to feel a little uneasy and David sensed that something was wrong. I tried to reassure him, "That's Dahlonega just below us, see the courthouse?" I was stalling because I knew I had gotten off course. About that time David came back with, "That's not Dahlonega, we're lost!" I did a 180 degree turn to take another look and spotted the water tower. Sure enough the name on the tower in bold letters was Dawsonville! I righted our course and headed toward Dahlonega and Wimpy Field. After nearly fifty years David and I can still laugh about the day he went flying with me. That would not be the last time Beetle flew with me as you'll see later in the book during our Vietnam tour.

The last week of May and the first week of June 1970 were packed with major life events for both Gerann and me. We graduated from NGC on 31 May, I was commissioned as a Second Lieutenant in the U.S. Army, and Gerann and I were married on 6 June. Goodbye NGC and hello life!

5. MARRIAGE

Gerann and I had been dating since February 1968 when we went to the Twerp Dance together. I'm not sure exactly when it occurred to me that she was the one that God intended for me. I wasn't a Christian in those days, even though I had been raised in a Christian Home. Nevertheless, on reflection, at some point I believe the Holy Spirit spoke to me concerning my relationship with Gerann and He gave me the inner assurance that Gerann was to be my wife. I knew that I loved her and that she loved me. I also knew that when I was with her I felt differently than I had ever felt before, a sort of warm glow.

In early December of 1969, I went to Rich's Department Store at Cobb Center in Smyrna, Georgia. I literally had no money but I was determined that I was going to buy Gerann an engagement ring. I picked out a beautiful diamond ring. It was a whooping ¼ karat! Best I can remember the cost was $250.00. I applied for a Rich's Credit Card Account and to my astonishment, I was approved!

My plan was to give Gerann the ring on Christmas Eve. This is when my family always got together at Mother and Daddy's to exchange gifts and celebrate Christmas together. We were all there, Cecil & Ellen with their kids, Joan & Clyde with their kids, Robert & Inez with their kids, Harold, Mother & Daddy and of course Gerann and me.

I had wrapped the small ring box and then I wrapped successively larger boxes placing the smaller one inside the larger one until the package was about three feet square. Gerann started to unwrap the large box with no idea what it contained. Each box was packed with newspaper and a note encouraging her to keep going. With each box she opened, the excitement was building. Finally, after unwrapping about six boxes she got to the one that had contained the ring. When she opened it, there was a note that said, "Close your eyes and hold out your hand." At this point she held out her left hand with the palm down as if expecting me to slide the ring onto her finger. I missed this cue; I turned her hand over and placed the ring in the palm of her hand and then she slipped it on and said, "I will!"

That was my somewhat awkward way to propose. The thought never entered my mind that she would turn me down. I was confident that fate had put us together; all glory to God, we've been happily married now for 49 years as of June 6, 2019!

Our Senior year at NGC was really fast. Gerann had finished her course work after fall quarter. She did her practice teaching during winter quarter at Clarkesville High School. During spring quarter, she lived off campus with Jan Walker and Peggy Mercer Rabb; they shared a three bedroom mobile home.

A very sad and disconcerting thing happened that spring. Peggy's husband, Robert Rabb, had graduated from NGC two years earlier and was now in Vietnam as a helicopter pilot. Late one night about 10 PM there was a knock on the door. A blurry eyed Peggy opened the door and standing there was a young Army Officer dressed in Class A uniform. He was accompanied by another officer (Military Chaplain). By this time Gerann and Jan were standing behind Peggy. Peggy knew before the officer began to speak. "Maam, I regret to inform you that your husband, 1LT Robert Rabb, was reported to have been killed in action by hostile enemy fire on 5 March 1970. On behalf of the Secretary of

Defense, please accept our deepest sympathy." Gerann and Jan literally caught Peggy before she hit the floor. This horrible turn of events did not bode well with Gerann or me. The fact that I was destined to be a helicopter pilot and most likely go to Vietnam was more prominent on both our minds.

Gerann got her first teaching job at Lumpkin County High School in Dahlonega teaching math during spring quarter 1970. Meanwhile, I was working at the Pizza Palace, Chow Hall, and the little grocery store one night a week. All the while I was doing all I could to make good grades in all my classes to insure that I would graduate on time.

After our engagement that December, Gerann was busy planning our wedding. We decided on June 6, 1970, which would be one week after our graduation at NGC and my commissioning as a Second Lieutenant in the U.S. Army.

We were married at Roswell First Baptist Church. My brother Robert was my Best Man. Groomsmen were Randell Cline, David (Beetle) Bailey, Chris Walker, and Tom Owensby. Gerann had as Maids of Honor her sisters Sharon Creel and Joy. Her Bridesmaids were Margaret Cline, Deanna Lloyd Owensby, and Lee Wallace. Reverend Brantley Seymour performed the ceremony.

Gerann was a beautiful bride and the ceremony was near perfect. I say near perfect because one small occurrence could have resulted in a catastrophe. Gerann and I had stepped forward to light the unity candle. Each of us picked up our individual candle and simultaneously lit the unity candle. We were then supposed to blow out our candle and replace the extinguished candle back in the candle stick. I blew mine out with no problem. I did not notice that when Gerann brought the candle near her face to blow it out her veil began to melt from the heat of the flame. Afterwards, my brother Robert, my Best Man, said that he was about to jerk her veil off but when she blew the flame out the veil also stopped its meltdown. That was a close one!

We planned to spend the night at the Royal Coach Motor Inn in North Atlanta and then leave the next day for a week-long honeymoon in Oklahoma City, Oklahoma. On our budget, we couldn't afford any of those exotic honeymoons so we planned to stay with Robert and Inez and do some sightseeing daily from there as our base.

Well as is the custom, especially in that day, my 'friends' had really done a number on my car. They had used black shoe polish on my white '66 Mercury Comet to write all sorts of cute phrases in addition to 'Just Married'. We were standing on the front steps of the church just before departing when my Daddy read one of the phrases that was written on the side of the car; *Roswell today, Hot Springs tonight!* Daddy turned to Mother and said, "They can't drive all the way to Hot Springs tonight." Mother promptly exclaimed, "Oh hush, Forrest!" My Daddy was good at unintentional humor. He once remarked about a gentleman that he had met, who happened to be a Rector in the Episcopal Church, "Yeah he's a well-educated man, and he's the Rectum of the Church."

We had a great honeymoon night at the Royal Coach Motor Inn. In that day, it was one of the fanciest hotels around. After a great steak dinner, we retired to our spacious room with a giant round bed. It was several cuts above your basic Holiday Inn!

The next day we drove to Kathryn and Melvin's (Gerann's Aunt and Uncle) house to pack for our trip to Oklahoma. I needed to wash my car so I asked Melvin if he'd like to ride with me to the carwash. He declined because he was watching a TV show. On the way to the carwash, it occurred to me that my car was 'dolled' up with *Just Married, etc.* and I thought, 'wow I'm glad Melvin didn't come with me!'

Gerann and I followed Robert and Inez in my Mercury with no air conditioning! It was over 800 miles and we drove straight through without spending the night. Back then, the Interstate Highways were not nearly finished so at least half the trip was two lane roads. In Memphis, I told Robert that I was about to fall asleep; he said, "Take this and you'll be fine." To this day, I don't know what that little black pill contained, but from Memphis to Oklahoma City I talked Gerann's head off.

We toured the Cowboy Hall of Fame in Oklahoma City and went to the city zoo. We enjoyed some great meals and generally had a wonderful time with my brother and sister-in-law.

We had been there about three days when I received a phone call from home. My lifelong friend, Chris Walker, was found dead! Chris had some emotional problems related to alcohol and the breakup of his marriage. Suicide was suspected but I was never convinced that Chris had voluntarily ended his life. The ride back to Georgia was not nearly as enjoyable as the ride out to Oklahoma.

I was a pallbearer for Chris. He was buried in Hollywood Cemetery next to his Mom's grave (she had died in her late 40s from cancer). Chris and I as boys had romped and played in the old cemetery looking for old graves and playing hide and seek. I couldn't believe he was gone. At that time, I was not a Christian though I believed in God, but the extent of my spiritual understanding was miniscule.

It was the middle of June; I had nearly four months before I would go on active duty at the end of October. I needed a job. Randell Cline's Uncle John was a foreman for Roadway Trucking Company. Their terminal was on Moreland Avenue in Atlanta. Randell spoke to Uncle John about me and I went to work on the dock loading and unloading trucks. The work was hard but the money was good; I made about $5.00 per hour working as an extra. I usually got in at least 35-40 hours per week.

One evening I was busy unloading one of the huge trailers all by myself. I was about halfway finished when one of the shop stewards strolled over and told me that I was working too fast. That's about the time I began to think that perhaps unions had outgrown their purpose.

Gerann and I rented an apartment on Gordon Road in Cobb

County. Gerann started her teaching job at Peachtree High School in August. We were doing great, enjoying life, and learning how to be married.

I quit my job at Roadway about two weeks before I had to report for active duty at Fort Eustis, Virginia. We had bought a '69 VW Beetle for Gerann. Later on, that VW Beetle would figure prominently in a trip from Mineral Wells, Texas to Laredo, Texas.

I kissed Gerann good-by and headed to Fort Eustis on 25 October 1970 in my '66 Mercury. I thought to myself, "I'm in the Army now!"

6. TOBC, FORT EUSTIS, VA AND PRIMARY HELICOPTER SCHOOL, FORT WOLTERS, TX

Driving to Fort Eustis on 25 October 1970, I listened to the Oakland Raiders beat the Pittsburgh Steelers 31-14. George Blanda was their backup quarter back; he was 43 years old and he had to go into the game because Darryl Lamonica was injured. Ole George led the Raiders to victory that day.

I was awestruck while driving through Williamsburg, Virginia; over the next several years Gerann and I would have the opportunity to become very familiar with Williamsburg, Jamestown, Yorktown and the entire Tidewater Area of Virginia. I would be stationed at Fort Eustis, Virginia three different times in four years. Whenever family or friends would come to visit, the historical tour was standard fare.

During the 600-mile drive from Atlanta, I wondered if Gerann and I had made the right decision for me to leave her in Georgia. She had started the school year as a math teacher at Peachtree High School and we decided that I would go to TOBC (Transportation Officer Basic Course) without her and that she would join me after the school year ended.

I signed in and received my BOQ (Bachelor Officer Quarters) assignment. My room was in a building that appeared to be circa 1950 or earlier. The plumbing was outdated and I had to share a bathroom with the officer next door. Each room had a door leading into the bathroom; inconvenient but I figured I could make do. A plus was that the Officer's Club was a short walk across the parking lot from my BOQ.

The first day of class I met several folks. I struck up a friendship with three single officers. Larry Hansen was a tall red headed man from Southern California. Dennis Burke was from Chicago, Illinois. Ira Silverman was a Jew from New York City. Along with me being from the Deep South, we made quite a foursome. We often went out to eat together and shared stories from our past.

Gary King, also an NGC Graduate, was in the TOBC Class one behind mine. Gary and his wife Judy would become some of our closest friends during those early days at Fort Eustis and later on as well.

Our country went through some turbulent times in the 60s and early 70s. We had dealt with the tragedy of assignations (JFK in 1963, MLK & RFK in 1968), the escalation of the Vietnam War during LBJ's administration, the promise of 'peace with honor' from Nixon and the eventual revelation of the Watergate debacle. In 1970, our military was in transition to say the least. Morale was at a low ebb because of the negative publicity surrounding the Vietnam War, discipline was waning, and our country was looking for some stability. Elimination of the draft was in the works with something on the horizon called 'VO-LAR'. This was the term used to label the All Volunteer Army.

Our TOBC Class was small, about thirty. There were at least three or four other classes rotating through at different points of the course. The Transportation School was an impressive building. Probably built in the 50s or late 40s, it was massive. Most of our training was in the classroom; we ventured down to the port and to an occasional motor pool for some hands-on activities. Our largest training exercise consisted of planning and executing a convoy from Fort Eustis to AP Hill and back. Each of us worked in small groups simulating a Company level staff. All the plans were submitted and then critiqued from the platform by the instructor. The end result was a melded convoy plan that the entire class had at least a small part in developing.

One of the requirements before graduating from TOBC was successful completion of the Physical Combat Proficiency Test (PCPT). This consisted of five events: 150-yard man carry; 40 yard low crawl; horizontal ladder; run, dodge and jump; and the one mile run. I had no problem scoring in the 90 percentile for each event and I usually scored 100 on the mile run. My buddy Ira Silverman was a hopeless plodder who was just not built to be a runner. I worked with him for about two weeks prior to the test and he made little progress.

Anyone who failed the PCPT would be recycled with the next class and after three failures you would be in jeopardy of losing your commission.

On the day of test, Ira had passed each of the four events leading up to the mile run with a minimum score of at least 70 on each event. The mile run was the last event. The minimum passing time was eight minutes. I quickly went to the front and finished well ahead of everyone else in about five minutes 30 seconds. As soon as I crossed the finish line, I turned around and ran back to Ira who was in last place! I ran alongside him, encouraging him to keep going. Each time he would slow to a walk I would get behind him and literally push him to start running again. On the last lap, about 50 yards from the finish line, we heard the timer calling out 7:50, 7:51, & 7:52. With about 10 yards to go I heard 7:58! I got behind Ira and literally pushed him across the finish line as we heard eight minutes. He had passed the mile run!

Gerann had joined me after Christmas. We rented a one bedroom apartment in Newport News. I graduated from TOBC on 15 January 1971; my flight school orders had me reporting to Fort Wolters, Texas in mid-April. What was I to do for three months?

I was assigned to the 355th Heavy Helicopter Company commanded by Major Tom Wolf. They flew the CH-54 Sky Cranes. I was to be the Tech Supply Officer. The unit was in the process of transitioning from CH-54 A Models to B Models. My task was to oversee the realignment of the PLL (Parts Load List). We were to transfer A Model Parts to the Georgia Army National Guard along with our CH-54 A Model Aircraft. In turn we were to order all the B Model parts for the new aircraft that we would be receiving. Little did I know that years later I would serve in the Georgia Army National Guard.

8 March '71 — Larry Hansen came over, we watched the 'Fight of the Century', Ali vs. Frazier. Frazier won in 15 rounds!

27 March '71 — Larry came over, we watched UCLA beat Villanova 68-62 to win the NCAA Basketball Championship.

On 1 April '71 Gerann and I pulled out for Georgia en route to Fort Wolters and Flight School. My '66 Mercury towed our '69 VW Beetle. We arrived at Kathryn and Melvin's (Gerann's Aunt and Uncle) house after about a twelve-hour trip. This would often be our 'headquarters' when we were in Georgia. Over the next twelve days we visited family and friends.

On 9 April we went to Pilgreens with James and Danny Bobo and their wives Marilyn and Debbie. This was one of the last times that I saw James and Danny. I recently reconnected with Danny Bobo after losing contact for about forty years. Unfortunately, I learned that his brother James is no longer with us. James succumbed to cancer several years ago. Danny and his wife are retired in Canton, Georgia.

We pulled into Mineral Wells, Texas at 9:30PM on 13 April 1971 after a two-day trip. The bed at the local Holiday Inn was a welcomed site. The next day we went looking for a place to live after I signed in at Fort Wolters. We rented a duplex apartment at 305 Northwest 25th Street. I would soon join the legacy of Fort Wolters as one of the many thousands of pilots that received their primary helicopter training there.

The Primary Helicopter School at Fort Wolters started with 125 Hiller OH-23 Raven helicopters. The number of helicopters peaked in 1969 at more than 1300, including the OH-13 and TH-55 types. Over 41,000 students, representing over 30 countries, graduated from the primary helicopter school during the 17 years it functioned in this capacity. Peak output occurred in 1967 with 600 students graduating each month.

Put in "mothballs" in November 1973, what was once known as Fort Wolters is now Wolters Industrial Park, housing a number of businesses, and in part of the old WOC area, a prison. (excerpts taken from Fort Wolters Chapter VHPA website) The U.S. Army Primary Helicopter Center and School Fort Wolters, Texas July 1956 — November 1973 Welcome to the Fort Wolters History Page, featuring a Then and Now Tour, compliments of chapter members Ira Will McComic and Jerry Barnes.

I had a few days before my Flight School Class would start so we took a side trip to Oklahoma City to visit Robert, Inez, and their kids. Larry Fenley was coming through on his way home so Gerann and I, Robert and Inez, and Larry went out to eat at Glenn's Steak House and later to Grand 35 Club. Larry, in keeping with his crazy reputation, tried to put a move on a black stripper. Fortunately, he was not successful!

I finally in-processed on 23 April; ran into Ed Acuff (NGC Graduate). Ed had been one of our best ROTC Flight Students back at NGC. When he told me that he was out-processing because he had 'washed out' of flight school that didn't help my confidence too much.

First day of classes was on 28 April. Our carpool was Gary Thompson, Jay Hamilton, Chuck Heldreth (NGC Graduate), and me. We all lived in the same neighborhood; there was a row of apartments across the street from our duplex where the Thompsons, Hamiltons and Heldreths lived. Our five months in Mineral Wells was exciting; we made some good friends and generally lived a great life. There was a little butcher shop near us and we would often drop in and have steaks 'cut to order'; that was some of the best steaks I've ever grilled even to this day!

Tom and Vickie Arnold were from Hooker, Oklahoma. Yep, that's not a typo, Hooker is really a town in Oklahoma. It's located in the panhandle and the land is flat as a table top. Tom was raised to be a farmer, wheat, maze, and corn. We had some great times with Tom and Vickie and are still close friends after all these years, even though we don't see them very often.

John and Cheryl Hirsh were from Yankton, South Dakota. We've stayed in touch with them and finally after many years we along with Tom and Vickie made a trip to South Dakota in July of 2011 to visit them.

Gary and Judy King divorced in the 70s after Gary was out of the Army. Gary has since remarried. Gary and his wife Joyce live in Etowah, North Carolina. We've reconnected in recent years and have visited one another several times.

There's more about the Arnolds, Kings, and Hirschs in my Dedication Chapter.

We lost contact with Jay and Nancy Hamilton after Vietnam. Recently, I got in touch with Jay. He and Nancy divorced many years ago but he has remarried. Jay and Marcheta live in Pensacola, Florida. We visited them at their Florida home a few years ago.

We've never heard from Gary and Marci Thompson since flight school.

During flight school, I had been in touch with Bob Stein. He was planning to do the Gainesville-Dahlonega Memorial Run for the second time and he wanted me to come back and run with him. I would go out to run five or six miles and it was tough in the West Texas dry heat! With the demands of flight school, I just couldn't find enough time to get into decent enough shape to make a 23 mile run. Reluctantly, I contacted Bob and told him he'd have to go without me.

There was a reception on 6 May at the Officer's Club to welcome the Vietnamese 'sister class' to our class. We were strongly encouraged to 'volunteer' to be a sponsor for a Vietnamese student. My little man was named Van (more on that later).

April 10—was my first day in the helicopter; a TH-55 nicknamed the 'Mattel Messerschmitt'! My IP (Instructor Pilot) was CPT Evans. He said, "You will learn as we go further into your training that we will usually be *flying low*; there's a reason for that. In Vietnam, the higher you fly the longer 'Charlie' (the enemy) has to get a good look at you." Consequently, about 2000 feet AGL (Above Ground Level) was the norm. We just did basic straight and level flight with a few turns; I tried to adjust my altitude with the cyclic, no, no! Altitude is controlled primarily with the collective. I was thinking this is going to be fun!

11 April—I tried to hover, wild! We got weathered out on 12 April.

13 April—Found the 'Hover Button'! Just my third day in the aircraft and I was hovering, I was ecstatic! The inability to hover was one of the primary reasons that caused 'washouts'. Hovering the TH-55 was one of the most difficult tasks I had ever accomplished. I had passed my first challenge, game on!

Several of us had planned a cook-out for our Vietnamese buddies. Jay volunteered to cook chicken on the grill. I had arranged to pick up Van at his barracks on post. I drove over and there he was sitting on the steps outside. In my best broken English I tried to communicate to him that it was time to leave for the cookout. After much persuasion and body language he reluctantly got in the car and off we went. We walked in and began to mingle with everybody. After a few minutes, Jay called me over to the side and said, "I think you got the wrong one."

The more I looked at my little man I realized that I had not picked up Van. I jumped in the car and went back to the Post; Van was sitting on the other side of the barracks. I motioned for him to come and he eagerly hopped in the front seat and off we went. So, I fed two Vietnamese students that day. I was a little embarrassed, but we all had a good laugh. I tried to explain to Van that all Vietnamese look alike to us. In his best broken English, he said "All American look like to me."

On 26 April I received my first Pink Slip, ugh, bad day! Just two days later, on 28 April, I soloed! I was so proud to pin my student wings onto my purple baseball cap. Each class had a different color hat to distinguish between classes. We were Class 71-44, purple hats.

Not long after I soloed, I was out on a local area flight west of Mineral Wells. You need to understand that West Texas all looks the same, especially from the air, small farm houses spotting the landscape, not many trees and even then very small and scrubby, quaint two lane roads many of them dirt and barely wide enough for one vehicle. I had been out for about an hour and it was time to head for the stage field.

During the peak of flight training at Fort Wolters there were 25 stage fields with names such as Ramrod, Sundance, Mustang, Qui Nhon, Hue, Bronco, and Vung Tau to name just a few. There were also two main heliports where all the helicopters were based and maintained, Dempsey and Downing.

Amid my exhilaration of being on my own in the West Texas Sky, I realized that I wasn't confident of which direction my stage field was. I began to weigh my options. I could wander around and hope to see something familiar to get my bearings, but that would be risky because my fuel was already getting low; I figured I had maybe another 30 minutes of fuel left.

I thought back to our initial safety briefing. We were told that if we ever had to land in the West Texas wilderness that we should find a good tree stump, have a seat and wait for an armadillo to happen by. Then just follow that armadillo and he would lead us to the nearest highway.

I decided that wasn't a good option so I swallowed my pride and keyed the radio, "Bronco, this is Trainer 637 (*tail number*), over." "637, this is Bronco." "Bronco, 637, I'm not sure which direction the stage field is." "637, Bronco, are you lost?" "Bronco, 637, negative, I'm just a little *disoriented* (a common expression used by many aviators when they are *lost!*)." Needless to say, I soon righted myself and found my way back to the stage field, although I did take a lot of grief from my fellow classmates once the word got out about my brush with disorientation.

Gary and Judy King went with us to Fort Worth on Saturday 5 June '71 to celebrate our first anniversary. We ate steaks at *Cross Keys Steak House* and then went to see *Escape From Planet of The Apes*.

David Bailey (Beetle) came for a visit on 21 June; we went to Bingo at the Officer's Club on Wednesday 23 June. I won a set of golf clubs, Gary & Judy won a Vacuum Cleaner, Tom and Vickie won a blender. We had a great night!

Next day I was scheduled for afternoon flight so Beetle and I played the front nine at Fort Wolters early that morning. My first ever round of golf. David had a 38 and I had a 67! But, I made a 40-foot putt on number nine for a par; I was hooked! Beetle left on Sunday 27 June; I played nine holes with Tom Arnold and Kevin, had a 55; better, think I'm gonna like this game.

Brother Robert flew into Dallas on Friday 2 July. On Saturday 3 July Gerann, Robert, and I went to *Panther Hall* in Dallas to see Leroy Van Dyke. There was a dance floor so Gerann and I had danced a few dances. A somewhat homely looking young lady with black horn-rimmed glasses came over to our table and asked Robert to dance. He reluctantly agreed and as they were waltzing across the floor she abruptly put her head up against Robert and stabbed him with her glasses! We joked about that many times through the years.

We met several people during our time in flight school. Dale and Linda Wells were from somewhere in Texas, I don't remember the town. What I do remember about them is that they were genuine Christians. Thinking back, they, especially Dale, had a positive influence on me. Dale was a couple of flight classes behind me and later after flight school he joined me in Vietnam as my assistant Platoon Leader.

On 10 July, Pepper Paulson and I played a little golf course in Weatherford, Texas. I had a 53 on the front nine and a 48 on the back nine. It was the first time I broke 50! Yep, I like this game.

My sister Joan and brother-in-law Clyde came for a visit on 11 July. Their boys, Jeff and Perry came along. We enjoyed cooking steaks on the grill and touring them around Fort Wolters, etc. Gerann went with them to Mexico while I stayed behind for school.

On 17 July, I broke 100 for the first time, shot 99! Yep, I like it.

Joan, Clyde, and Jeff left on 17 July. Perry stayed with us until 31 July. We took him to Love Field in Dallas for flight to Atlanta. When the plane landed, he rushed off and went directly to the restroom passing Joan and Clyde in the process. He didn't know there was a restroom on the plane!

We were beginning to think about the move to Fort Rucker, Alabama for the Advanced Phase of our flight training.

Gerann, me, Gary and Judy made a side trip to Laredo, Mexico 13-15 August. We went in our '69 VW Beetle and we had all sorts of trouble with the AC, engine running hot, etc. In spite of that, we had a great time, spent the night in San Antonio and toured the Alamo on the way down. Of course we all bought souvenirs in Mexico. Gary and Judy bought a piñata and we had to make the return trip with the sun roof open in order to fit everything in! We looked like the "Beverly Hillbillies" going down the highway.

Gerann and Nancy Hamilton left for Fort Rucker on 19 August to look for places to live. Gerann put down a deposit on a townhouse in Ozark, Alabama, Clentown Manor.

We had our graduation from Primary Phase of flight school on 27 August. I finished 16th in a class of 52. We pulled out of Mineral Wells at 9:40 AM heading for Alabama and rolled into Ozark at 11:15PM exhausted! I thought, man I can't wait to get into the Huey!

7. ADVANCED HELICOPTER SCHOOL, FORT RUCKER, AL

On Sunday, 29 August 1971, Gerann and I drove to Macon, Georgia. We went to Aunt Clara and Uncle Franklin's house. Aunt Clara was a great country cook. We had a feast with all my favorites, i.e. fried okra, green beans, and homemade peach cobbler. My parents, Joan and Clyde, Jeff and Perry were all there, I'm 23 years old today. We drove back to Ozark that evening and celebrated my birthday with Gary and Marci Thompson.

The next day I in-processed at Fort Rucker and our household goods and furniture arrived so we began to set up our townhouse.

In processing was delayed so I finally got it done on Wednesday 1 September; classes don't start until after Labor Day on 7 September. I played golf on Wednesday afternoon and on Thursday. Gerann and I left for Atlanta on Friday afternoon. We had a great time visiting with all the family; our headquarters was Kathryn and Melvin's house. We bought our first color TV from Rich's, a 19 inch MGA; also saw Randell and Margaret Cline.

7 September—First day of classes and orientation ride in the Huey; I thought wow, this was like going from a Model-A (TH-55) to a Cadillac (Huey)! A couple of weeks later I made 83 on my first check

73

ride, not bad, most of my classmates had similar results, word is the IPs (Instructor Pilots) don't like to give everybody a case of the "big head" too early. Next day I almost aced the first test (94), I'm on my way to becoming an Army Aviator!

The drudgery of Flight School can be demanding, both physically and mentally. Flag Football proved to be a great outlet for some of the stress that builds up without you even knowing it's there. We Purple Hats beat the Red Hats in our first game 13-0. Once everyone found out that I had played center in high school and at NGC I was "type cast" at that position; oh well, at least I get to touch the ball on every play.

On Friday 17 September, we had a "training holiday", no classes and no flying. I was looking forward to a round of golf at the beautiful Fort Rucker Course. I woke up early, about 4AM, with excruciating pain in my side and back! I didn't know what was going on but I knew I had to get some relief. Gerann drove me to the hospital emergency room on post. I was hurting so bad I couldn't stand erect. No matter what position I tried there was no relief. The nurse on duty began to tell me that I would have to go to another building and get my medical records, etc. I looked up into her eye from my crouched position and said, "Lady, I'm not leaving until you do something to give me some relief from this pain!" After I got on the floor and started crawling around like a wounded dog, she realized that I was in fact having unbearable pain. They wheeled me into a back room on a gurney and gave me a shot. In a very short time I was in "La-La Land" and thankfully feeling no pain! Later, I was told that I had been given a shot of morphine! They sent me home with a urinal and a strainer. That weekend I managed to catch my first kidney stone; this would be the first of eight; about every one to two years from that point I birthed another stone. This continued until about 1981 and then strangely it stopped until I finally had another one in 2007. Hopefully, now I'm past kidney stone birthing age.

I bounced back pretty quickly. There was a party on post at the Lake Lodge the next night and then on Sunday I played 18 holes at the Silver Wings Course on post. A bunch of us watched the Falcons-49ers Game in the clubhouse; Falcons won 20-17!

Flying in the early days at Rucker was up and down. I'd have a bad day followed by a good day. This was typical especially in the Huey which I transitioned into on 29 November. The touch on the controls of the Huey was much more sensitive than the TH-55 and the OH-13. We would spend the first few weeks in the OH-13 (this is the Bell Helicopter that everyone is familiar with from the Movie and TV Series M.A.S.H.) Our early instrument training was in the OH-13; we flew numerous hours under the hood. This was a gadget that you put on much like a hat with a large bill which enabled you to see the instrument panel but prevents you from seeing outside the cockpit. I, like most others, hated it.

We won our second Flag Football Game 7-0. Gary Thompson caught the winning touchdown. Center Screen went for a first down but it was called back for a penalty.

1 October 1971: I had a great day flying, getting the "hang of it"! My thoughts were, "I can't wait to get into the Huey". Gerann's parents, Red and Florence, and her brother Tommy arrived late for the weekend. On Saturday I played 18 holes at Silver Wings with Red. This would be the first of many rounds of golf that I enjoyed with Red and he usually beat me; today I had a 103 and Red a 91.

My brother-in-law, Clyde Carson, dropped in for a visit later in the month; he brought me a desk. He, Gerann, and I had supper at El Palacio's Mexican Restaurant; this was one of many meals that we enjoyed there. It's sort of ironic that we ate more Mexican food in Alabama than we did in Texas.

Dale and Linda Wells came in later during October (24 October);

Dale was a couple of flight classes behind me. We became friends in Mineral Wells. Later Dale would serve with me in Vietnam as my assistant platoon leader in the 18th CAC.

My brother Harold came for a visit on 4 November; he stayed three nights. We showed him around Fort Rucker; he really enjoyed the aviation museum. I leaned on him pretty hard about his smoking in the house; other than that, we had a great time, cooked out pork chops (his favorite), watched Georgia beat Florida 49-7 on TV. We talked about old times on *"gobblers' knob"* (that was slang for the neighborhood we were raised in; actually it was meant to be *"gossipers' knob"* but over the years the mispronunciation evolved into *"gobblers' knob"*).

Judy Burgess was from Opelika, Alabama. She and Gerann taught school together in Ozark, at the Middle School. Her husband Jim was a Vietnam veteran and a helicopter pilot. The four of us made a trip to Atlanta 13-14 November. We got rooms at Mark Inn near *Six Flags Over Georgia*; the girls shopped while Jim and I watched Georgia lose to Auburn 35-20; that one really stung since Jim was a huge Auburn fan! The anticipation of the game was hyped nationwide. Both teams were undefeated. Auburn was ranked 6th in the nation and Georgia was ranked 7th. Auburn's eventual Heisman Trophy winner, Pat Sullivan, threw four touchdowns as Georgia went down to defeat "between the hedges".

The next day we went to Atlanta Stadium and watched the Falcons lose to the New York Giants 21-17. We had a great time with Jim and Judy even though the football games didn't go the way I would have preferred.

I hated Instrument flying (more on that in the Vietnam chapter). It was one of the most difficult things I had ever tried to master. Your body and mind will play some horrible tricks when you must depend entirely on what you see inside the cockpit without ground reference. Everybody struggled with this. I had a bad flight on Monday but then on Wednesday with Captain Shuman as my IP (Instructor Pilot) everything was much better, getting the hang of it! Big check ride on Friday; Jesse and Barbara Blanco came over for supper on Thursday night; Jesse and I studied afterwards while the girls went to a PTA meeting at Gerann's school.

Friday 19 November—Made 83 on my Check Ride! Next week is gonna be short, just two full days and half day on Wednesday then off four days for the Thanksgiving Holiday!

Joan, Clyde, Jeff, and Perry arrived on Wednesday. We had a great time with them, shopping, El Palicio's for Mexican, Officers Club for Bingo, Aviation Museum, etc. Joan and Clyde helped Gerann cook Thanksgiving dinner. Over the years, we all have laughed about one incident that wasn't funny at the time. Gerann cooked the Turkey in a bag; this was very popular at the time. Something didn't work right and that bird came out dry as a bone! Fortunately, there was enough broth and after bathing it several times in the broth the turkey was revived and all was well with our dinner. To top things off, Georgia squeaked by Georgia Tech 28-24 at Grant Field; it wasn't supposed to be a close game but at least it kept our record with just one loss at 10-1.

Back in that day the Officer's Club at Fort Rucker was "state of art". They didn't skimp on anything. We were treated to special nights such as Beef & Burgundy, Shrimp Fest, and of course Bingo. The Grand Prize was always something amazing, such as a Cadillac fully loaded or a Cessna 172 (a four seat single engine airplane)!

There was also the Lake Lodge. This was the site of numerous parties, dances, etc. during our time at Fort Rucker. Aviators studied hard, worked hard, flew hard, and partied hard!

29 November: Finally, my first day to fly the Huey; it was awesome! The Huey's more advanced technology was a dream to fly compared to the ancient TH-55 & OH-13. I would compare it to the difference between an old manual typewriter and an electric one. Later on, once I mastered the feel of the controls; I could hover up to a big Southern Pine Tree and pick off Pine Cones one a time with the rotor disk! (Looking back now, this was no doubt a dangerous thing to do but it was a great confidence builder).

3-5 December: Long weekend; we stayed with Kathryn and Melvin as usual. We did some visiting, ate dinner with Mother and Daddy at 1240 Sizemore. Gerann shopped with Kathryn and we visited Joan and Clyde. On Sunday, we met Gary and Judy King; we all went to see the Falcons beat the Raiders 24-13. The game was great but the weather was horrible, rain and cold.

During our time in flight school we met some great friends, some of which we have kept up with until this day. We would have friends over for meals and vice versa, we'd get together for games such as Scrabble, Jeopardy, cards, etc. Also, we would eat out frequently at several restaurants; El Palcio's seemed to be the one we most often enjoyed. It was a great time with lots of fond memories. Here's a partial list of some of those friends: Gary and Marci Thompson, Jay and Nancy Hamilton, Bill and Linda Bryan, Jesse and Barbara Blanco, Jim and Judy Burgess, Tom and Vickie Arnold, Gary and Judy King, John and Cheryl Hirsh. We have kept us with the Arnolds most through the years. Back in July of 2011, Tom and Vickie met us in Kansas and the four of us made a trip to South Dakota to visit John and Cheryl Hirsh; that was great fun. Recently, we have reconnected with Jay Hamilton who remarried several years ago. We have enjoyed getting to know his wife Marcheta and rekindling our friendship with Jay. We have also kept up with Gary King over these many years. He too remarried a number of years ago. We had the opportunity a few years ago to meet Gary's wife Joyce when we and several other NGC graduates gathered in the Military Department to dedicate some *Joe Cline Art Work*. Additionally, Gary and Joyce spent a couple of nights with us in July of 2018. The four of us attended the annual convention of the Vietnam Helicopter Pilots Association (VHPA) in Atlanta. One highlight of that was the opportunity to fly as a passenger in a vintage Huey at the Army Aviation Heritage Foundation (AAHF) located in Hampton, Georgia near Atlanta. There are many others that I've wondered about and this birthed the idea of a flight class reunion for Class 71-44. We had that reunion in October of 2017. Fourteen of our classmates gathered in Nashville, Tennessee along with our wives for a three day weekend of fun, food and most of all fellowship. A very special memory of that trip was at the Grand Ole Opry. Country Music Legend John Conlee recognized our group. He instructed the stage manager to raise the house lights and the entire crowd of over four thousand gave us a thunderous standing ovation! This was truly a touching gesture. Many of us had tears of joy running down our cheeks and cold chills going up our spine.

10 December: After a week and half, today I soloed in the Huey! We had several days when we were 'weathered out' or this day would have come much sooner. The fun really starts now. I've already touched on the difference between the early trainers we flew and the Huey but something else deserves to be mentioned here. The UH-1, Huey, built by Bell Helicopter, is undoubtedly the most durable, most reliable, and safest helicopter ever designed and put into service. This was proven during the span of the Vietnam War in extreme weather conditions and all sorts of combat roles, i.e. combat assaults, combat resupply, aerial reconnaissance, MedEvac, and many other innovative uses which are too numerous to mention. I have often thought that we should have coined the nickname *Timex* for the Huey because *'it takes a licking and keeps on ticking!'*

Our social life during flight school was nothing short of awesome! Everyone developed close friendships, many of which are still being fostered today more than 45 years later. The following is a chronology of what I'm referring to.

11 December: I played nine holes of golf with Pepper Paulson; later Gerann and I went by the Paulson's to see their new baby. That evening Gerann and I went to Jim and Judy Burgess' house for a party. Judy and Gerann taught school together at Ozark Junior High. Jim was not in my flight class; he was a Captain who had already served a tour in Vietnam and was now stationed at Fort Rucker.

12 December: Jesse and Barbara Blanco came to our place for dinner.

13 & 14 December: Night Flying this week, cool.

16 December: Gerann, me, and Gwen (one of her teacher friends) went to El Palicio's for supper. Gerann and Gwen went to a PTA (Parent Teacher Association) meeting.

17 December: We were released early for the Christmas Break. Gerann and I went to the PX (Post Exchange) and then to Daleville Steak House with Gary and Judy King for supper. Afterwards we all went to their place for drinks and Jeopardy.

18 December: Another trip to the PX and then to Dale and Linda Wells place for supper. Dale was a couple of classes behind us. I don't recall exactly how we met but later on Dale was assigned to my unit (18th CAC) in Vietnam as one of my test pilots in the maintenance platoon; he sort of served as assistant platoon leader.

20 December – 2 January 1972: Took a long leave for Christmas. We visited family and friends and did our traditional Christmas things.

We made a quick trip to Oklahoma 27-30 December to visit my brother Robert and his family. Back in Atlanta we spent New Year's Eve with Randell and Margaret Cline at their place. Finally, back to Ozark and Fort Rucker on 2 January. In about four weeks I'll be getting my wings!

8 January 1972: Had one of my last check rides today before graduation, 87. IP (Instructor Pilot) was a little tough but we were warned that would be the case because they didn't want us getting a "big head"

13 January 1972: A bad tornado hit Enterprise, Alabama and the surrounding area today. There were eight Hueys damaged at Lowe Field. The worst news came when I learned that Bill White (fellow NGC classmate) lost his wife in the storm. Bill was not in my flight class but was stationed at Fort Rucker as permanent party. He was on duty as Officer of the Day when the storm went through the trailer park where he and his wife lived, very sad day.

14 January 1972: Gerann drove to Valdosta to get her sister Joy and Mike McKinney, her steady boyfriend, for a weekend visit. They were in school at Valdosta State College. Joy and Mike would marry in September of 1972 while I was in Vietnam. We took them to the Aviation Museum, ate out a couple of times and watched the Super Bowl on Sunday 16 January. Dallas beat Miami 24-3. Miami would get redemption the next year by going undefeated and winning Super Bowl VII over Washington 17-0.

17 January 1972: Most of our classmates received their orders today for their next assignment after flight school. The majority of our classmates were going straight to Vietnam after graduation. Several were going to Cobra Transition and then to Vietnam. Four of us, John

Hirsch, Tom Arnold, Gary King and me had orders for Cobra School, AMOC (Aircraft Maintenance Officer Course) and then Vietnam.

27 January 1972: Took my last written test in flight school today; now the pressure is off and nothing but smooth sailing until graduation!

28 January 1972: I went to Enterprise and Dothan to look at new cars. My '66 Mercury Comet has a bunch of miles and no A/C. Gerann's VW Beetle is not too reliable and also the A/C isn't working.

29 January 1972: Graduation Party at the Lake Lodge was wild. Not everyone came but with the wives we had a good crowd of forty seven. Needless to say we "let our hair down" and a good time was had by all!

3 February 1972: Last day of flying. Just a routine flight around the local area. All tests and check rides are done and we're just marking time until we get our wings.

4-5 February 1972: We made a quick trip with Gary and Judy King to Savannah to scout for a place to live during Cobra school. It's a short school, but there's plenty of renters who cater to each class that comes in every 4 to 5 weeks. We rented a one bedroom efficiency apartment about three blocks off Abercorn behind Oglethorpe Mall. We're set!

7 February 1972: Brother Robert and his wife Inez arrived at 0630 after driving all night from Oklahoma City so they could be there for my graduation. Over the years it's always meant a great deal to me that they made such an effort to be there for me. They went to bed and got some badly needed sleep. Later that night we all went to the Grand Ball at the Officer's Club. Afterwards several of our friends came to our place for drinks. We didn't get into bed until well after midnight but it was an amazing night.

8 February 1972: This is the big day. We all got up early and Gerann fixed a good breakfast. Graduation started at 0830, early but that's the Army way. It was over in about an hour. I was overjoyed when Gerann pinned my wings on my chest. Ten months of hard work along with highs and lows along the way was finally over. I was now officially an Army Aviator! To celebrate we grilled steaks that night and had a wonderful time with Robert and Inez.

11 February 1972: I had been dickering with Bill Parrish, a salesman for Nichols Olds, for about a week on the price of a gorgeous '72 Olds Cutlass Sport. We finally closed the deal. It listed for $4,529 and I made the deal at $3,872. My pay as a second lieutenant was decent but I certainly couldn't pay cash. I financed it for 36 months for something like $145 per month. The car was perfect, dark green with a light green vinyl roof. The engine was a 350 Cubic Inch V8. I opted for the automatic transmission and had the dealer install cruise control which was a relatively new option back then. Wow, we had a really cool car now!

12-15 February 1972: The last few days were filled with clearing post, packing and making final arrangements for the move to Savannah and then on to Fort Eustis later.

16 February 1972: I'm excited about Cobra School even though Gerann can't go with me at this time. She had to stay behind and finish out the quarter at Ozark Middle School. Her principal is giving her a hard time about leaving in the middle of a school year. I've been tempted to give him a good chewing out but I've held my tongue. I left Ozark at 0800 and rolled into Savannah around 1545. I began to think about flying the AH-1G Gunship. If the Huey was a Cadillac then the Cobra must be a Corvette! Man I can't wait to get into one of those slick looking flying machines.

8. COBRA SCHOOL & AMOC

17-26 February 1972: It was a long 10 days without Gerann. All our friends took real good care of me. I was invited for supper almost every night to either the Arnolds, Kings, or Hirschs. Also I ran into one of my high school buddies, Larry Roebuck. He and his wife had me over a couple of times as well.

22 February 1972: First day of class in Cobra Hall. Following four hours of classroom instruction we got our first ride in a Cobra that afternoon. Sad to say but I got a little light headed riding in the front seat. I was okay until the IP did a 90 degree rollover and then I almost lost my lunch, ugh! Gary King fared even worse. They had engine failure over Interstate 95 and the IP actually did an emergency landing (auto rotation) onto the expressway. There's more about this in chapter 12. Gary had another close call during our time in ROTC Flight Training at NGC. He and his instructor were on final approach to Wimpy Field. As they cleared a stand of pine trees off the end of the runway the aircraft (Cessna 150) was hit with a violent downdraft. Gary's instructor immediately took over the controls and managed to bring the aircraft under control less than 100 feet off the ground, narrowly escaping a nose first crash.

23 February 1972: Had my first night flight in the Cobra. Shooting approaches from the front seat was awkward. The cyclic is not between your legs. Instead it's on your right side and just a little stub. I couldn't get the feel of it and consequently all my approaches were below standard. I went home a little disappointed but not defeated.

24 February 1972: Second night flight. I'm beginning to get the hang of it now, much better. We'll probably move to the back seat (pilot's seat) soon.

25 February 1972: We had class all day until 1700. Tom Arnold and I ate supper at McDonald's and I left around 1900 for Ozark. I arrived at 1AM Central Time, whipped!

26 February 1972: We pulled out at 1715 for Savannah. Gerann drove the Cutlass. I led the way driving my Mercury Comet and pulling the VW Beetle behind. We really had a caravan going down the highway. After a long drive we arrived in Savannah at our little apartment at 1:00 AM, tired!

27 February 1972: We slept late, 0930, went to KFC for lunch and then I hit the books most of the afternoon. Man there's a lot to learn about this "Corvette"!

29 February 1972: Jerry Paul, Gary King, and I had a long study session while watching the Glen Campbell Show.

2 March 1972: First check ride and I didn't do well. Disappointed but not defeated.

3 March 1972: Made a 94 on written test, better! Beetle arrived at 1530. We went to the Pirate's House for Dinner, good eatin'.

4 March 1972: Beetle, Jerry Paul, and I played a round of golf at the Hunter Golf Course. I need to mention that Jerry Paul was a good guy from east Texas and his wife Nancy was a sweet lady. We got to know them better during Cobra School and really enjoyed their company. Unfortunately, I learned years later that Jerry passed away, I believe in his early 50s from cancer.

6 March 1972: Beetle left early and we ran errands most of the day. We watched the Sonny and Cher Show with Jerry and Nancy.

9 March 1972: Night flight, getting better.

11 March 1972: I love weekends! Jerry, Tom, Kevin, and I played nine holes of golf. Gerann and I ate steaks at Jerry and Nancy's house and then we all went bowling on post. Everybody bowled back then. Every military base in the world has a bowling alley. It's cheap entertainment and keeps the soldiers close by.

12 March 1972: Went to Williams Seafood Restaurant with Larry Roebuck and his wife Carolyn. Back then Williams was the place to eat seafood in Savannah.

13 March 1972: It didn't go well today during my flight. I'm thinking maybe I'm not cut out to be a "Snake Jockey". I called Nichols Olds in Enterprise. When I waxed the Cutlass I discovered a definite spot in the middle of the driver's door. It appeared they had attempted to repair a "ding" rather than paint the entire door.

14 March 1972: Check ride today went well, I got an 84. That was about average. Most of the IPs were tough and they demanded perfection. Bill Parrish called today. Nichols Olds will pay for the repaint of the door. I took it to Fuller Olds, the local dealer in Savannah.

Cobra school was anomalous throughout the four weeks. Each time I had a success it was quickly followed by a failure or something less than desirable. This was the case with most of our classmates. The fact that we were rushed through the process in just four weeks would account for some of the staggered progress that most of us experienced.

Once we started the gunnery portion we would fly the short distance to Fort Stewart to do our shooting. Armament consisted of 2.75" rocket pods mounted on the wing stubs and two 7.62mm Miniguns or two 40mm M129 grenade launchers in the turret. When we set up for a gun run we would come in at about two thousand feet AGL (above ground level), slow your airspeed to 50 knots and then dump the nose over toward your target. The airspeed would build quickly as you punched your rockets off. By the time you pulled out of your dive at 500 feet AGL the airspeed would be 180 knots! As you pulled up out of the dive those long, wide rotor blades (wider than a Huey) would slap the air with a loud popping noise that almost sounded like another round of armament firing. Once we finished our gunnery portion of the flight we'd climb to 2000 feet AGL and head for Savannah and Hunter Army Airfield (HHAF). Navigation wasn't a problem. There were a couple of paper mills along the Savannah River just north of Savannah. You'd just look for the large cloud of smoke billowing from those plants and make a beeline toward the smoke and smell!

16 March 1972: Grades for our last written test were posted; I made 98, surprised myself. There was a simple Graduation Ceremony held at 1600. We received a certificate and were deemed Cobra rated pilots.

Now it's time to refocus on the next task at hand, AMOC (Aircraft Maintenance Officer Course).

22 March 1973: After taking a few days leave to visit family and friends we officially signed out at Cobra Hall and departed for Fort Useless (Eustis) at 10AM. We arrived in Williamsburg at 2130 and decided to get a room there.

The next several days were spent settling in, looking for a place to live and in processing for AMOC. We settled on a one bedroom apartment in Horse Run. This was about 20 minutes from post on Mercury Boulevard.

31 March – 2 April 1972: We made a quick trip to Richlands, Virginia to meet Randell and Margaret Cline there. Randell was from that area of Virginia. We spent a couple of days visiting his family and enjoying some good Virginia mountain cooking. Randell took me by his old high school and we all went to church on Sunday in Grundy, Virginia.

6 April 1972: Started classes today. This is not gonna be easy. We're going to study every system of the UH-1 Iroquois (Huey). When we graduate we'll be certified test pilots and maintenance officers. It's interesting to note here that of all the aircraft deployed during the Vietnam War, the Huey was the most dominant. There were about 12,000 Hueys used during the duration of the war and over 5,000 of them were destroyed. There's a good reason Vietnam has been called the Helicopter War.

In the early days of AMOC, I toyed with the idea of trying out for the Post Track Team. I was still a decent runner then. I made a few practice sessions and even bought a pair of expensive track shoes. I soon realized that I was just chasing a dream. AMOC presented all the challenges I could handle with all that it entailed.

9-11 April 1972: Bill and Linda Bryan came for a visit on his 30 day leave prior to departure for Vietnam. We toured Williamsburg, ate some great seafood, and had a wonderful time visiting with them. I wouldn't see Bill again until our flight class reunion in October of 2017.

We studied hard to learn all that was required of us but we managed to find time to relax and have fun. Weekends were filled with trips to the Officer's Club, golf, bowling, and always great food in some amazing restaurants. One place stands out among all the rest. Nick's Seafood Pavilion in Yorktown was awesome! More than once several couples would make the short trek to Nick's and we were never disappointed. The view of the York River was breathtaking and the food was absolutely top shelf.

18 April 1972: Most of our instructors were retired military. Of course they were older men but with a great deal of experience. Today we had "Pappy"Thornhill on the podium. He was a hoot, very entertaining and easy to listen to. Best I can recall he covered electrical systems of the Huey. Unfortunately, many of our classes were boring and methodical. Nevertheless, we had to soak up all that we could.

We were overloaded with technical information, most of it very detailed. I bought a cheap cassette tape recorder. The method I devised went like this: I would take copious notes, record the notes along with excerpts from selected TMs (Technical Manuals) and then lie on the bed at night while I listened to myself. I would listen to my recorded notes on my way to class each morning. This gave me about 20-30 minutes additional study time, depending on traffic.

22 April 1972: Lazy Saturday. Gerann and I went to the movies at the Beechmont. We saw *The Last Picture Show*. That same movie was the first one I saw in Vietnam and the last as well. I'm not sure that had any great significance but it is an interesting coincidence.

23 April 1972: We ate supper with John and Cheryl Hirsch. Apollo 16 had been in progress since 16 April. Astronauts John Young and Charles Duke had been on the lunar surface since 20 April. This was the fifth successful landing on the moon (Apollo 13 of course had to abort their landing and return to earth using the Lunar Lander as a "life raft"). Many folks had already become blasé about the lunar missions but I was still intrigued by it all. The four of us watched with anticipation and excitement as they successfully blasted off from the moon. There would be just one more lunar mission after this. I have always thought that we should have forged on with space exploration at that time. Instead the space program took a back seat for many years.

Lunchtime was always interesting. We usually got at least one hour and sometimes longer depending on the class schedule. Occasionally several of us would pile in one car and drive to Buck's. This was a local club/restaurant located near the front gate on Mercury Boulevard. The food consisted primarily of burgers, dogs, fries, etc. The attraction was the entertainment. They usually had Go-Go Girls dancing on stage to popular songs of the day. I can still hear Lynn Anderson singing *Rose Garden* blaring through loud and clear on their huge jukebox. Looking back, the girls had more clothes on than what you see at most beaches or local pools today.

26 April 1972: First test today, 76, gotta do better than that!

2 May 1972: We had our first graded PE (Practical Exercise) yesterday. I left thinking that I had probably busted it. When the grades were doled out I had an 88, I'll take that.

6 May 1972: The Arnolds, Kings, Hirschs, and us went to Neil Diamond concert at the Scope in Norfolk. We had a great time and Neil really put on a fantastic show.

91

15 May 1972: During an outdoor rally in Laurel, Maryland, George Wallace is shot by 21 year old Arthur Bremer. Wallace was making his third run at the White House. This essentially ended his campaign and he remained wheelchair bound for the remainder of his life. It seemed to me another senseless act of violence. Similarly, the assassinations of JFK, RFK, and MLK all fit into that same category.

Oftentimes we would find ourselves in front of the TV when Johnny Carson came on. Usually we'd be with at least one or two other couples. It seemed everyone was a fan of JC. One of the most hilarious guests I remember was on 19 April 1972. I don't remember the gentleman's name but he was a manualist. In other words he played music with his hands. He would clasp his hands tightly together and then begin to squeeze air out. It was remarkable and funny at the same time. Over the years we've laughed many times about the manualist.

25-28 May 1972: Long weekend for Memorial Day. We went to Georgia to visit family. As normal, we stayed with Gerann's Aunt Kathryn and Uncle Melvin in Atlanta. My nephew Jeff was graduating from Greater Atlanta Christian School so we were able to be there for him. Good food and quality family time abounded with both our families. Melvin and I slipped away on Saturday night to a local pool hall and played a couple games of eight ball. Of course we had a draft beer or two. Little did I know at the time I would eventually become a teetotaler.

30 May 1972: Back to the grind of AMOC. Lunch at Buck's helped break the monotony for several of us.

3 June 1972: Jack McElreath (Mac), Gerann's uncle, was in Norfolk for 30 days temporary duty with his shipyard job out of Charleston, SC. We spent the day with him, Navy BX, Virginia Beach and out to supper. Jack was in the Navy during the Cuban Missile Crisis. He was on a nuclear submarine as part of the naval blockade. I always liked Jack and wished we could see him more often.

6 June 1972: Second Anniversary! Sammy's Steak House for early dinner and then Sonny and Cher Concert at Hampton Roads Coliseum. Arnolds, Kings, and Hirschs all went with us. It was an amazing concert, what a show!

7 June 1972: Jack Mac spent the night with us. We had a great time talking, laughing, and catching up. After Johnny's monologue we hit the sack.

8 June 1972: Major Benoit from Officer Personnel in Washington paid our class a visit. His message to us, no orders are being changed, we're all going to Vietnam.

18-22 June 1972: Red and Florence, Gerann's parents, along with Tommy, spent four days with us. We watched Jack Nicklaus win the U.S. Open. This was his third U.S. Open victory and his eleventh major championship. Eventually he would win eighteen majors, a record that still stands today.

Jack's wife Shirley had joined him. They came over on Monday and we had a great time of food, fun, and fellowship. I grilled steaks and we laughed and talked late into the night.

Unfortunately, it rained much of the time that Red and Florence were with us so we didn't get to the golf course. We did manage to take them to some of the sights. I had class but Gerann took them to Williamsburg and Jamestown. They left for Georgia on 22 June.

25 June 1972: We went to church with Dale and Linda Wells and their little boy Ty. At that time I wasn't too interested in spiritual matters. Thinking back, I realize that Dale was trying his best to be a good witness for me and to encourage me. I didn't know it at the time but Dale would land in my unit in December of that year in Can Tho Vietnam.

28 June-4 July: Sister Joan and her two boys, Jeff and Perry, came for a visit. Clyde couldn't come because of business. We did all the regular events locally. A highlight of their trip was a day trip to Washington D.C. We hit all the monuments, Arlington Cemetery, Unknown Soldiers Tomb, etc. It was a long day but everyone enjoyed it.

9 July 1972: A bunch of our friends went to Virginia Beach. Gerann's Uncle Jack, wife Shirley, and their son Mike (4 or 5 years old) all went along. We were having a fun day at the beach and suddenly it all turned sour. Mike was lost! We feverishly started looking for him. Of course we notified the life guards and anyone who would listen. His mother, Shirley, was a nervous wreck. After about 30 minutes one of the life guards came walking up with him. Wow, instant relief! It seems that he was walking toward his parents and got distracted just for an instant. That's all it took to get him off course so he began walking along the beach, hopelessly looking for his Mom and Dad. Sadly, that incident put a veil over an otherwise spectacular day.

The next five days were filled with making arrangements for the move to Georgia. Gerann will stay there while I'm in Vietnam. All our test scores were in and all that we were waiting on was graduation day.

14 July 1972: Graduation was early morning, a quick ceremony and now I'm a school trained maintenance officer and test pilot.

We pulled out for Georgia at 1130 and arrived at headquarters, i.e.

Kathryn and Melvin's at 2330. I had sold the Mercury to nephew Jeff so I drove the Cutlass with the VW dragging behind.

Gerann and I had decided along with Gary and Judy King that we would rent a house together while Gary and I were in Vietnam. This made a lot of sense. We could save money by sharing expenses, i.e. rent, utilities, etc. We found a house in Decatur on 1973 Rosewood Drive. I thought that was somewhat prophetic since we'd be coming back in 1973. Another odd thing about the house was that it was just around the corner from where Randell Cline's Aunt Rosie and Uncle John had lived. They had moved a couple of years earlier. It would have been nice to have Uncle John close by to look out for the girls.

18 July 1972: Gerann and I bought a new bedroom suite at Sheraton Galleries in downtown Atlanta for $419. The chest of drawers from that suite still survives. Our daughter Stephanie has it in the guest bedroom of her and Patrick's home in Sugar Hill, Georgia.

22 July 1972: Gerann and I, along with Gary and Judy, did the town! We went to the Nitery Club and saw Morganna. Ronnie Allin (NGC classmate) and his wife Eugenia were there too. Next was the Regency Hyatt House, Domino Lounge, and finally to the Varsity!

Gerann and I planned to fly to the west coast about one week before my port call. We will spend a week in San Francisco before I have to leave. Our flight was scheduled for 13 August.

In those three weeks we packed a lot in. Of course we spent some quality time with family first and foremost. There was a trip to Fort Rucker to reminisce. We spent a night in Daytona Beach and went to the dog races. Next was Disney World for a couple of days then onto Port Malabar. We had bought a lot in the General Development Corporation community of Port Malabar during flight school. We bought another one! From there we went to Cape Kennedy and the Space Center. We spent the night in Cocoa Beach and slept on a water bed before heading to Charleston. We spent one night with Jack and Shirley and then back to Atlanta, whew!

We arrived back in Atlanta on 9 August and the next four days was a whirlwind tour. First night we went to dinner with Robert and Inez. Afterwards, the four of us dropped by Marion and Freida Pinnell's. I mentioned Marion earlier because he was Robert's closest friend and my scout master in the Explorer Scouts.

10 August 1972: The next day was a visit to my parents where my sister Joan and her husband Clyde were there along with Robert and Inez.

11 August 1972: A visit to Larry Fenley's parents, Lonnie and Lois, and then to RJ Gazaway, Robert's father-in-law. We sat around and had a few cold beers with RJ, Robert, and Walker Kitchens (one of RJ's other sons-in-law).

12 August 1972: A huge picnic at Mountain Park with all the family! Afterwards we went by Kathryn and Melvin's and then to 1973 Rosewood to meet Gary and Judy's parents.

13 August 1972: The day has arrived. We catch our flight to San Francisco tonight. Brother Cecil came by to bid us farewell. Robert, Inez, Marion, and Freida drove us to the airport.

14 August 1972: Good flight. We arrived in SF at 2:00 AM. We caught a cab and rolled up in front of the Cartwright Hotel at 3:30 AM, tired!

We slept until 9:30 AM, gotta get at it, too much to do in a short amount of time. We walked to the Cannery, Ghirardelli Square, and Fisherman's Wharf. Then we hopped on the cable car back to the hotel. After lunch we walked down Powell Street to Market Square.

15 August 1972: Up at 10:30 AM, breakfast at the Hofbrau, rode the trolley to Telegraph Hill and Coit Tower, walked back through Chinatown and ate dinner at #9 Fisherman's Grotto.

16 August 1972: Rode trolley to Golden Gate Park, toured the Japanese Tea Garden, dinner at the Hofbrau, then to topless and bottomless Broadway (wild to say the least).

17 August 1972: We slept late and then took the Cable Car to Ghirardelli Square to shop for souvenirs. We had a great lunch at Café Portofino. Later that afternoon we hopped on a Grey Line Bus tour to the Muir Woods. The giant redwood trees are astounding! I could hardly believe what I was seeing.

Later that evening back in SF we had a scrumptious dinner at the House of Prime Rib.

18 August 1972: I put Gerann on a plane heading to Houston at 8:00 AM. We said our goodbyes but it was tough knowing I would not see her for a long time. We kissed, embraced, and reluctantly parted. Her plan was to meet up with Barbara Blanco in Houston. They were planning to spend a couple of days together. This was well before cell phones. Barbara didn't show; somehow they miscommunicated. Gerann happened to have Nancy Paul's phone number. Nancy came to the rescue and Gerann had an enjoyable couple of days with her before flying onto Atlanta.

19 August 1972: Gary, John, and I ate breakfast at the Canterbury Hotel. We went to Fisherman's Wharf and took a Bay Cruise. Later that evening we rode a bus out to Travis Field. We left the "World" at 2230 Pacific Time. We had stopovers in Hawaii, Guam, and the Philippines. I thought to myself; this is it, I'm on my way to the Vietnam War.

9. VIETNAM (FLIGHT PLATOON)

The coastline of Vietnam slowly began to come into focus out the right side of our charter TWA (Trans World Airline) aircraft as we approached from the Northeast. We thought we saw plumes of smoke to the north of the capitol city. Saigon was an enormous city sprawling below us as we lined up for our approach into Ton Son Knut Airfield and Camp Alpha. All U.S. Military personnel at this time of the war processed in and out of Camp Alpha. The pilot made a steep approach staying at 2,000 feet AGL (above ground level) until the last half mile and then he descended at a rapid rate so that we would be exposed to possible ground fire the least time possible. It was a ride that would rival any amusement park roller coaster!

We stepped onto the tarmac at 1200 hours on Monday 21 August 1972 (Gerann's birthday). The air felt almost dirty as a heavy layer of smog had the entire field draped in moisture. The temperature was in the high 90s and the humidity was at least 90%. The wet season runs from May to November so we were just about in the middle of the season in mid-August.

I called David Bailey (Beetle), one of my closest friends from NGC days, from Camp Alpha. David was assigned to MACV (Military Assistance Command Vietnam) Headquarters there in Saigon. He met Gary King, Tom Arnold, and me at the Officers Club for drinks. David

99

suggested that I could stay with him until I received my assignment. He had a room downtown in a hotel. MACV had rented the entire hotel, about eight stories high, for some of their military personnel. David said he had plenty of floor space and that I could set up a cot and camp out as long as I needed to.

Two days later, on Wednesday, I hopped a Huey for a short ride to Long Bien where I had to report in to receive my assignment. The Captain in charge was Skip Bell, another NGC Graduate! My assignment was the 164th Aviation Group in Can Tho.

I started In-processing on Friday 25 August at Camp Alpha. In-processing was typical Army, hurry up and wait. I had my personnel records and as we processed through, each of us was anxious to get the 'paper work drill' finished and get on to our units. You had the feeling that the sooner you got started with your mission and were busy then the days and months would pass and you'd be home before you realized. The Paris Peace talks had been on again, off again since 1968. There was much anticipation that we would soon reach an agreement with the North Vietnamese which would mean an end to the war that had raged for over ten years.

Nevertheless, we were all soldiers and bound by our oath of office to carry out orders to the best of our ability. We would do that regardless of what the politicians decided until we were told differently.

I asked the Captain in charge how was I supposed to get to Can Tho? He said, "See that building over there? That's flight operations; go over there and find out when there's a 'bird' going south to Can Tho and put your name on the manifest." The young specialist working the flight desk said there were no flights scheduled for Can Tho in the next few days and that I should check back daily until there was.

David had to work each day and I rode in with him to Camp Alpha to check on flights to Can Tho. After the third day, I began to wonder if I would spend my entire tour 'ghosting' in Saigon. David showed me the sights, which didn't take long. We were careful to not venture too far into the city. Viet Cong were everywhere so you really never knew exactly who the enemy was. The same Vietnamese man that served you lunch may slide under the wire and try to cut your throat the same evening. This was always a problem, identifying the enemy that is. Of course that's always been the case in every war that was ever fought, but Vietnam carried it to new heights.

One day we went to the Army Hospital and visited with Jim & Bill Crissey. They were both in our graduating class at NGC and since they were both Medical Service Officers they were assigned to one of the largest Army Hospitals outside the United States. Bill and Jim were both First Lieutenants, same as David and I, but they were in Captain slots. That was commonplace, especially toward the end of the war. Because we were in a drawdown preparing for the eventual cease fire, many Junior Officers and NCOs found themselves in positions one or two grades above their current rank. It definitely forced you to grow up quickly or you would fail miserably. Most grew up fast and performed admirably. We had lunch with Jim and Bill and reminisced about the good ole days at NGC even though we were only a couple of years removed from our Alma Mater.

Finally, I had a flight scheduled to Can Tho for Tuesday out of 8th Aerial Port at Ton Son Knut. Can Tho was located about 75 miles south of Saigon in the Delta Region of the country.

My last night in Saigon, David suggested that we could go up on the roof and watch the movie. It seemed that the USO (United Services Organization) usually showed a movie each evening. There wasn't much else to do so most of the soldiers would meander up and take in the movie of the evening. That night 28 August 1972, I watched "The Last Picture Show" with Van Johnson, Cloris Leachman, Jeff Bridges, and a very young Cybill Shepherd. It was in black and white and as I sat watching, I thought, "I sure hope the title is not prophetic!"

29 Aug 72: We were up at 0515 hours. David (Beetle) drove me to 8th Aerial Port. I was a passenger on a UH-1H (Huey). We went skids up at 0800 hours. Normally Can Tho was about an hour but the weather was awful, low ceiling, raining, and less than one mile visibility. After a harrowing 90-minute flight, we were on final approach to the airfield at Can Tho. At about one mile out I could see the outline of the city of Can Tho along the banks of the vast Mekong River. The base at Can Tho was on the north end of town. There were two gates on the base with access to the city. The perimeter around the airfield was guarded with primitive fencing with concertina wire across the top and bottom. There were sand bagged bunkers spaced about 50 yards apart with openings for fields of fire right and left. As part of the anticipated handoff to the ARVN (Army of Vietnam) we shared responsibility for securing the airfield. The ARVN had about one third of the perimeter and we had the rest. As the airfield came into clear view, helicopters could be seen on both sides of the runway. They were parked in revetments (thick concrete walls about five feet high) designed to protect them from shrapnel in case of incoming mortars.

I walked into the 164th Orderly Room and placed a copy of my orders on the clerk's desk. He glanced at me and then my orders and said, "We didn't know you were coming." I thought to myself, "I could have stayed in Saigon and nobody would have ever known the difference". He asked me to wait. After a few minutes, he came back and said that I was to report to the 18th Corps Aviation Company (CAC) on the other side of the runway. Our unit was located on the north side of the runway. The consolidated Mess Hall was on our side, along with most of the other support services. On the south side of the runway were the CAV unit and the Headquarters for the 164th AV Group.

Major Jerry Childers, 18th CAC Commander, was about six feet tall, flat top haircut and about 32 years old. This was his third tour in Vietnam. He had briefly looked over my personnel record and commented on the fact that I was Cobra (gunship) qualified and a graduate of AMOC (Aircraft Maintenance Officer Course). AMOC gave me the designation of Aircraft Maintenance Officer and Test Pilot. Major Childers said that he would put me in a flight platoon where I would fly combat support missions. At this point in the war, Vietnamization was well underway; all the U.S. combat units had been withdrawn. We were in the process of turning the war over to the South Vietnamese military. Most of our missions were single ship in a combat support role. We did a little of everything including Medical Evacuation (Medevac), resupply, aerial reconnaissance, and general 'ash and trash' missions. Before I left his office, he commented that I should not get too comfortable in the flight platoon because I would probably be needed later in another capacity.

I was shown to my hooch, a private room about eight feet x seven feet. It was one of four rooms in the same building with two on each end. The latrine (bathroom) was next door in a metal Quonset hut. There was just a short walk to the officer's club, a very small bar with several tables and a makeshift stage for live bands. A small game room in the back provided entertainment with a pool table and a ping pong table.

30 Aug 72: I was up at 0800 hours; went to see the Flight Surgeon about getting my clearance to fly (this was Standard Operating Procedure, SOP, when reporting to a new unit). He was on R & R (Rest and Relaxation). I went by the Maintenance Hangar and had a good conversation with the Maintenance Manager, CPT Zec. He was 'short' and I figured the chances were pretty good that I'd get his job when he went back to the 'world' (home).

One of the first folks I met was Marshall Eubanks. Marshall was 'short' (due to go home before Christmas) and he sort of took me under his wing and showed me the ropes. The first thing Marshall helped me with was hiring a 'Momma San' (someone to clean my hooch, take care of my uniforms, etc. She was about twenty and actually quite attractive. Marshall explained that she, as well as the other 'Momma Sans', worked for several people so that the going rate per month was about 2500 Piasters (five US dollars!) This is what I got for five dollars a month: cleaned my room and made bed daily, spit shined my boots, starched and pressed my jungle fatigues, and washed my flight suits; what a deal!

4 Sep 72: My first mission was with CPT Cook. He was a veteran aviator on his second tour. He told me that *flying low*, no higher than 2,000 feet AGL (Above Ground Level), was the recommended altitude. He said, "That keeps you out of small arms range." I would soon discover that on occasion NOE (Nape of the Earth), especially flying in the Delta with practically no trees for natural cover, proved to be beneficial. My first mission was nothing exotic, just 'ash and trash' missions to Vinh Long and Chu Long. We logged about six hours, landing at a couple of firebases north of Can Tho to resupply with 'beans and bullets'. The base at Vinh Long was on a branch of the Mekong River. This was most memorable because our landing pad was a dock next to the road along the river bank. We had just enough room to fit our skids onto the dock with about three feet clearance on either end. Needless to say, this was somewhat tricky, especially with a stiff crosswind. After several flights to Vinh Long, this dock landing became routine. My 'target practice' on pine cones in South Alabama came in quite handy as dock landing required a sure hand on the cyclic and collective and a deft touch with the feet on the anti-torque pedals. We did take small arms fire on take-off out of Chu Long but they missed. I had decent supper in the chow hall, got six letters from Gerann (they finally caught up with me), and watched *The Cowboys* with John Wayne in the Officer's Club. My thought was, "Maybe this is gonna be OK."

5 Sep 72: First mission to Cambodia today. When we had a Cambodian mission, we'd take a roll of masking tape to the flight line. On the tail boom are the words *United States Army*. We had to tape over the word *Army*; you see our politicians back home were telling everybody that our military was not flying missions in Cambodia. After we crossed into Cambodia, the U.S. Army Colonel in our back seat gave us a set of eight digit coordinates. We were to land (hover at three feet without touching our skids); Cambodian soldiers ran out to our aircraft, papers and maps were exchanged and then we were on our way. Now we could land at the International Airport at Phenom Phen. I was amazed as we talked with the tower operator in English and then listened as he talked with Air China, Air France, and ARVN (Army of Vietnam) aircraft in their own language.

Jim Ayers was a 'cowboy type pilot'. He was very proficient but at the same time he had a definite swagger that belied his professionalism. Jim had been in SOBC (Signal Officer Basic Course) with David 'Beetle' Bailey. I had the opportunity to fly several missions with Jim and, to say the least, it was always interesting.

9 Sep 72: Flew with Marshall Eubanks today. We flew to Dong Tam which used to be a large base about 35 miles southwest of Saigon. Toward the end of the war there were just a few separate units there, i.e. Navy River Rats and some ARVN Units. We had lunch there and prior to taking off for Can Tho, we got word from the U.S. Advisor that the VNAF (Vietnamese Air Force) had a "Bird" (Helicopter) shot down with an SA-7 just north of Dong Tam about one hour earlier. The VC (Viet Cong) were notorious for employing those shoulder mounted heat seeking missiles. On our flight back to Can Tho, both Marshall and I had our heads "on a swivel" looking for the tell-tale white smoke stream that was the signature of the SA-7.

10 Sep 72: Flew the west coast with CPT Poore. There was a lot of fighting in the province of Tinh Bien along the coast between ARVN Troops and VC. We landed at a small hamlet near Tri Ten and Frank Maxwell (NGC Class of '69) jumped onto my "bird"! He was working with the local ARVN as a U.S. Advisor.

11 Sep 72: Today was my first experience with MARS (Military Aux-iliary Radio System). I managed to talk with Gerann for about five minutes. Each time we'd finish our part of the conversation we'd have to say "over". It was very frustrating and cumbersome. That was the only time I used MARS.

13 Sep 72: Flew with CW2 Bob Addington today. We had the Senior Military Advisor in our back seat (a US Army Colonel). We received a call for help from an ARVN Outpost (OP) south of Rach Gia which is located near the coast of the Gulf of Thailand southwest of Can Tho. They had been under siege from the VC (Viet Cong) all night and were in bad need of resupply and MEDEVAC. The VNAF (Viet-namese Air Force) had been called but failed to show. The Colonel asked Addington and me if we would take the mission. I had been in country a little over three weeks and here I was being asked to go into a situation where we were most certainly to be exposed to massive enemy fire and risk losing our whole crew and perhaps our aircraft as well. I looked at the Chief and he asked, "Well, what do you think?" After a moment of reflection, I said, "Well, I guess that's what we're here for."

As we approached the landing area just outside the OP, you could see clearly the VC surrounding the entire perimeter. Addington and I were both on the controls (this was SOP when you expected enemy fire; that way if one or the other sustained an injury that would prevent him from flying then the other pilot would take full control). We were

coming in with a glide path steeper than normal and as we descended
we both began to shrink down as low as we could into our armor-plated
seats so as to gain maximum protection. We were at 100 feet AGL and
not a single round had been fired, strange I thought. We took it all the
way to the ground and as we touched down I observed several dead VC
all around. An ARVN Officer ran out and told us he had 24 wounded and five KIA (killed in action). We would have to make two lifts.
They put on a couple of stretchers first and then the 'walking wounded',
women and children began piling on. In a matter of a couple of minutes
we had people packed in like sardines and more wanting to go.

Finally I said, "We gotta go!" Addington started pulling pitch and
easing the cyclic forward. I was lightly on the controls in case something happened to him. Those who couldn't get on the aircraft were
holding onto the skids, we weren't going anywhere unless we could get
free. I instructed the crew chief and flight engineer (each one sitting
in the well on each side with a mounted M-60 Machine Gun) to start
stepping on hands so they'd turn loose. We started gaining ground
speed but with the high-density altitude and our overloaded condition,
I wasn't sure that we'd be able to hit Effective Translational Lift (ETL)
and get airborne. Our skids were literally dragging through the rice
paddies and at last we approached airspeed of 15-20 knots and with a
shudder of the main rotor we hit ETL! Again, even though we could
clearly see VC all around the OP, we did not take a single round. Once
back on the ground at the Province Capital of Rach Gia, I counted as
our passengers began to get off our 'bird'. There were ARVN soldiers,
women, and infants; I counted 34 human beings that got off our Huey!
No wonder we nearly crashed in the rice paddies!

We went back for a second lift to get primarily just the five KIA
and a couple of stragglers. Most had gone on the first lift.

Over the years, I've recalled that day many times and wonder why
the VC did not fire a single round at us. Perhaps The Good Lord was

looking out for us and He just intervened long enough for us to get the wounded, women, and children out of there?

18 Sep 72: Flew with CPT Chaney to Moc Hoa, the province capital. This was strategically important because it was the largest population center between the Cambodian border and Highway 4. It was well within reach of NVA (North Vietnamese Army) 105mm artillery located in Svay Rieng Province. Our mission consisted of taking the Province Chief and the Senior US Army Advisor on their weekly 'errands' around the province. Chaney was OK but I hoped I wouldn't draw him again during my tour. I suspected he probably had a large number of mirrors in his hooch.

26 Sep 72: Flew with CW2 Hensley to Rach Gia. We had two chaplains on board and carried them around to various outposts. Apparently, they were training the ARVN chaplains. We were flying south of Rach Gia east of a canal at 2,000 feet AGL when we came under fire from a 37mm cannon. The aircraft pitched up about 20 degrees but we weren't hit. We nosed it over and pulled pitch all the way up under our arm. That's the fastest I ever flew a Huey; we were topping out near 120 knots.

27 Sep 72: Day off, I needed it after the 37mm incident yesterday. I rode with Marshall Eubanks as a passenger to Saigon and Ton Son Knut. He had some sort of 'ash and trash' mission and I figured it would give me something to do. I called Beetle; he met me at the helipad. We were going to take off and kill a couple of hours in Saigon but his jeep wouldn't crank so we walked over to the PX (Post Exchange), ate a late lunch, and went back to the helipad. He said he'd try to get down to Can Tho soon and spend a couple of days. We got back to Can Tho around 1800 hours, ate supper at the O Club, had a few beers, and called it a day.

During the time I was gone (about eight months), I'd write Gerann almost every day. In turn she would write to me daily; sometimes I'd get as many as six letters in one day. The mail wasn't too reliable. When that happened, I'd lay them out according to the postmarks and read them in order. Mail was a very big thing then unlike today with E-mail, Facetime, etc.

I tried to run at least three or four times a week; Eubanks would often run with me before he went back to the 'world'. Staying in shape was one motive but I believe the main reason was to break the monotony. On days we had off, it would get boring, even though we had a little Officers Club to help us with our morale. The primary thing was that you just missed being home with your loved ones. Small things like being able to run out for a hamburger or just enjoying a day driving in the country were sorely missed.

7 Oct 72: The perimeter defense around the airfield was shared 50/50 with the ARVN. I drew guard duty for the next nine days! As Officer of the Guard it was my job to check all the bunkers in our sector periodically during the night. I had a jeep with a driver for the duration of my duty.

The first night on one of my rounds as I approached one bunker, I was not challenged. I walked to the rear of the bunker and to my surprise both soldiers were sound asleep. I didn't wake them. Instead, I gathered up their M-16 rifles, carried them to the jeep, went back, and then woke them. They both sat up with a shocked look on their face and began scrambling to their feet and simultaneously looking for their rifles. It looked like something straight out of a *Three Stooge's* movie. When I began to question them about their rifles and why they were not alert, I got my point across. I pulled nine straight days as Officer of the Guard; those two soldiers were both awake and alert after that first night each time I checked their position.

I was Officer of the Guard until 16 October; pretty boring duty.

Fortunately, there were no incidents of any VC trying to probe our perimeter. However, Colonel Alverson did catch the guard on position B-1 sleeping on my last night. This was not the same bunch I caught earlier so there was little said about it.

20 Oct 72: David (Beetle) had said he was coming early today but he didn't show; he screwed up his schedule. I was sitting in the Officer's Club and in walked Beetle around 1945 hours! He bunked in with Jim Ayers who he knew from his Signal Officer Basic Course.

21 Oct 72: I had the day off so David and I slept late (0820) and after breakfast in the mess hall we went downtown to Eakin Compound. I had to coordinate with Group regarding some upcoming missions so David went along and we killed some time in town afterwards window shopping. I kept my distance from all the locals especially the small children. I was always careful to protect my wallet and valuables when off our compound after what happened to me on my initial venture downtown. On my first trip downtown I was the victim of adolescent pickpockets. A group of kids fleeced me of my wallet, watch, wedding ring and college ring!

22 Oct 72: I flew with Jim Ayers today. We had "ash and trash" mission with a US Colonel and a Province Chief in our back seat. I told David that we'd probably be back mid-day and that he could hang out in the Officer's Club. That didn't sit well with him so he said, "Why don't I just go along with ya'll?" I looked at Ayers and we both nodded OK but with the caveat that if we got in a spot and didn't have room for him then we'd have to "bump" him. (In other words, leave him). He agreed to that. As fate would have it, we found ourselves about 40 miles south-west of Can Tho in a small hamlet along a canal and we took on several passengers which left us one seat short. I told David that we'd be back to get him as soon as possible. He sure looked bewildered and sad as we took off headed for Rach Gia, the capital of Kien Giang Province. We finally got back about an hour later and as we landed Beetle came running with about a dozen Vietnamese kids chasing after him. He jumped in and yelled, "Let's go!" We weren't sure what the problem was but David explained that he had been keeping the kids at bay with bubble gum and that he was down to his last piece.

That evening we went to the Officer's Club. There was a hail and farewell for those leaving and the new arrivals. We had free steaks and nickel beer. David, Jim, and I were sitting at a large table with two or three other officers. We had at least twenty beers sitting on the table and everyone was having a rollicking good time. I reached for another can and as I did I accidently tipped over an open can and some beer spilled on the sleeve of the officer sitting next to me. I said, "Oh man, I'm sorry." He said, "You should be more careful." He proceeded to pop the top on another beer, leaned over and poured it up and down my entire right sleeve. I just sat there. When he was finished, I slid my chair back, popped the top on another can, walked around behind his chair, pulled his shirt collar back and poured the entire contents down his back. That did it. For the next twenty minutes or so it was complete bedlam! Everybody got into the act. We were throwing beer on everyone and in a matter of minutes we could hardly stand up because of the slippery mess on the floor. It took us about an hour to mop up all the beer and put the club back in decent order.

25 Oct 72: Had a Cambodia mission today with CPT Ham. We had a US Colonel in our back seat (don't remember his name). The weather was marginal, overcast and intermittent rain. After we had crossed into Cambodia the Colonel came on the intercom and said he thought he'd seen something and asked us to do a 180 degree turn to have a look.

We were at 2,000 feet AGL. Visibility was poor but we could definitely make out a tank and two or three APCs (Armored Personnel Carriers) backed into the tree line on Highway 2. There were also troops scurrying around trying to hide. This was at least a company sized unit of Khmer Rouge, the communist backed regime that was attempting to overthrow the existing government of Cambodia. Eventually they did overthrow the government in 1975 under their ruthless leader Pol Pot. This resulted in what became known as the Killing Fields when over two million innocent people were slaughtered.

We dialed up the radio frequency of CAS (Close Air Support) which was being provided by Navy A-4 fighter bombers off the coast. We circled at 2,000 feet until they arrived on station in about 10 minutes; two A-4s. They radioed that because of poor visibility they couldn't make (see) the target. The Navy pilot said, "I need you to fly down and drop smoke on the target." I immediately asked him to re-peat his request. CPT Ham as the PIC (Pilot in Command) took the controls, we dropped down to about 500 feet AGL, I leaned out the right window, pulled the pin on a red smoke grenade and let it drop right on top of their position. All the while, we were taking multiple rounds of small arms fire. Fortunately, they couldn't rotate their big guns quick enough and we were out of there as fast as that little ole Huey would take us; about 120 knots which is fast for a Huey. When we landed at Phenom Phen, to our surprise upon close inspection of the airframe we had not sustained one single hit. I saw CPT Ham a couple of days later in the mess hall and he told me that the Colonel had put us both in for a DFC (Distinguished Flying Cross). Later, when the awards came in, CPT Ham got his DFC and the Lieutenant (me) had been downgraded to an Air Medal with 'V' Device (Valor). I wasn't too upset at the time but as I discovered later on that rank has its privileges in awards as well as other things. Only thing I've said about that incident over the years is that the last time I checked; I was sitting in the seat right next to the Captain.

Peace talks had been going on sporadically since 1968, but to no avail. Lately there seemed to be some possible breakthroughs on the horizon.

To deal with the unsolvable problems in Paris, President Nixon directed Henry Kissinger, his National Security Advisor, to start secret one-on-one meetings with Le Duc Tho, a member of North Vietnamese politburo, in August 1969. However, those secret meetings and negotiations faced the same trouble as the talks in Paris. Three years passed by with little progress from both sides. A major breakthrough came on October 8, 1972. After disappointing results of the Easter Offensive and the fear of political isolation if the U.S. could reach rapprochement with China and Soviet Union, Hanoi made concessions and expressed its willing to consider a peace agreement as long as a free election and political reform were included. In late October 1972, a draft of the treaty was unveiled by Kissinger. (http://thevietnamwar.info/what-was-paris-peace-accords/)

On the evening of 27 October, Major Childers called a meeting to discuss how a possible peace treaty would affect us and to answer questions about how we would handle moving out. I've been in the Army two years today.

The next day, on 28 October, I flew with CWO O'Conner in the vicinity of Soc Trang. We had a request for assistance from an ARVN OP (outpost) NW of the village. They had been receiving small arms fire during the day and asked that we do a recon by fire around their base. We circled several times and emptied several hundred rounds of M-60 machine gun ammo. If there were any VC in the area I believe we 'encouraged' them to leave.

31 October: Halloween was a bad day! I flew with Addington. Our mission was in the vicinity of Mi Tho, which was about halfway between

113

Saigon and Can Tho. We had a CH-47 Chinook with 17 on board (12 from 18th CAC and 5 from other units) shot down earlier that day with an SA-7 heat seeking missile. We hovered over the crash site, no survivors, just a huge black spot, sad.

On the way back to Can Tho, we could see a big storm brewing in the distance. Two thunder heads were forming about ten miles to the south. We had an opening so we pulled the collective up under our armpits and leaned forward, getting our airspeed up to 110 knots trying to split the two thunder heads before they came together. We didn't make it! In an instant, we were totally IFR (Instrument Flight Rules) with zero visibility and no ground reference. I took the controls from Addington and went 100% IFR depending wholly on my instruments, attitude indicator, turn and bank indicator, altimeter, etc. We were in the 'soup' for at least ten minutes but it felt like 10 hours. We finally broke through but still had minimal visibility all the way back to Can Tho. The training I had received in flight school and the fact that our class, 71-44, was the first to graduate with an IFR ticket definitely saved my life and the lives of all our crew that day. In retrospect, I can see clearly that was another time that The Lord was looking out for me.

On top of everything else that happened to us, we found that we were under Red Alert when we returned to the airfield. I slept in a revetment (two raised concrete walls) until 0400 (4 AM). I thought, man these peace talks are getting rough.

1 November: I flew with Sims today. We took small arms fire north of Ben Tre, no hits. We were still under Red Alert, I thought wow, these peace talks are killing us.

3 November: I flew with O'Conner for the second day in a row. We took small arms fire on take-off out of Ca Mau. When we returned to

Can Tho, I dug an AK-47 round out of the armor-plated seat that I had been sitting on. That seat saved me from being shot in my *kester*!

4 November: Easy day of flying around local area in tail number 711 & 714 with Addington. We made a short flight to Bac Lieu, mostly 'ash and trash'. We enjoyed some local cuisine (*dink* food). It was pretty good and I didn't get sick, still have no idea what it was? Red Alert again at 2400 hours; I got tagged for Bunker Augmentation Force. I took Eubanks place because he had a sore big toe.

8 November: 'Tricky Dick' won re-election by a landslide!

9 November: I woke up at 0300 hours sick as a dog, vomiting my guts out. Went to the dispensary at 0700 and they gave me something for nausea. I was in bed all day, 'Wonder if this was a delayed reaction to the *dink* food a few days earlier?'

12 November: I flew with Rob Myer today in Dong Thap Province which is located along the Cambodian border. This was a "hotbed" of enemy activity and one of the primary centers for Khmer Rouge Activity as those communist forces were building for what would become "The Killing Fields" later on, in 1975. There was heavy fighting between ARVN and a mixture of Khmer Rouge and NVA troops. I was barely breathing most of the day; the 'pucker factor' was rather high. "I need a break!"

13 November: I'm off until 16 November so I called 'Beetle'; going to Saigon tomorrow for RON (Remain Overnight).

14 November: I left on the 'Mail Bird' for Saigon at 1000 hours; we arrived at 1120 hours and 'Beetle' met me at the helipad. We had tacos for lunch then went to Personnel; ran into Ray Barbee there who was my bunk mate at Advanced ROTC Camp, Fort Bragg, in 1969. Man, it's a small world. Ray was a great guy and a Clemson graduate. In Chapter 4, I mentioned Ray but I'll recap it here. I took him "under my wing" that summer of '69 at Bragg. Being from a "party" school, Ray knew very little of military matters so I showed him how to spit shine boots, make military corners on his bunk, break down his M-14 Rifle, etc. In short I helped him all the way through camp. At the end of the six-week camp, I finished second in my 40-man platoon. Ray Barbee finished first! Ray, Beetle, Bill Hardy and I went to supper downtown Saigon. 'Beetle' picked up the check!

15 November: We flew back to Can Tho around 1400 hours. There was a '*Gook*' band in our Officer's Club; they weren't too bad.

16 November: After two and a half months of flying combat support missions that totaled 250 hours of flight time, I got the word today that I'm moving to the Maintenance Platoon tomorrow as the Platoon Leader and AMO (Aircraft Maintenance Officer). It's a Captain slot but in these last days of the Vietnam War it was not uncommon to find Lieutenants filling Captain and even Major slots as we began the final drawdown prior to the end of the war. This will be good experience for me to be in charge of a 40-man Maintenance Platoon. Among my responsibilities will be recovery missions and test flights. Before too long. I would add two test pilots to my platoon. I am excited about the possibilities that lie before me, but at the same time I am somewhat apprehensive.

There's one story that I can't find an entry for in my calendar but it's just too remarkable to leave out. On one of David's visits to Can Tho, we didn't have much to do on the weekend. Missions had begun to wind down and you can only play so much pool and ping-pong before you begin to lose interest. I talked with the Captain (don't remember his name) in Flight Operations and he agreed to schedule a mission on Sunday to Vung Tau (the In Country R & R Center) which was on the coast of the South China Sea. I put David in the right seat, which was usually where the "Peter Pilot" (second in command) flew and off we went to Vung Tau. We had no crew and of course Beetle was not a rated pilot. Thinking back, it was probably a dumb thing to do and fortunately I'm well past any statute of limitations regarding misuse of government property. Nevertheless, David and I had a great time at the beach that day. I landed right on the beach, tied the blades down and we had a blast enjoying the sights and sounds of beach activities. The Vietnam War was a million miles away! I flew us back that evening with no incident and to this day we both reminisce about the day we had our personal aircraft for a trip to the beach.

10. VIETNAM
(MAINTENANCE PLATOON)

17 November: SFC Faust was a man of average height, about 5'9", dark tan and muscular and probably in his late 30s. He was on his third tour in Vietnam and on first impression appeared to be somewhat unsure of his young First Lieutenant (Me) who had just been placed in charge of "his" Maintenance Platoon as the new Platoon Leader.

We sat down and had a good open and frank discussion. SFC Faust began to loosen up a bit when he realized that I was not going to come in and make wholesale changes without regard for his expertise as the grizzled veteran he was. After all, with things winding down as fast as they were, SFC Faust, as the Platoon Sergeant, had been pretty much running things for several weeks prior to CPT Zec's departure as the Platoon Leader.

This was a great opportunity for me to grow as a military leader and to gain some valuable experience as the Aircraft Maintenance Officer of a large aviation company in a combat zone. I have always considered the Officer/NCO relationship in a command situation to be similar to a ship. The Officer Leader acts as the rudder setting direction and making course corrections when needed. The NCO Leader acts as the engine; he is the one who makes the organization go, pushing the junior leaders and holding them accountable. The Officer Leader must have trust in his NCO Leader that he will get the job done and accomplish the mission. Interference from the Officer Leader is only warranted when the "ship" strays off course.

Our platoon consisted of forty of the most professional soldiers I've ever been associated with. We never had a mission cancelled due to unavailability of mission capable aircraft.

18 November: I am quickly getting into the flow of being a Platoon Leader. Soldiers automatically think that the "Ole Man" (normally a term reserved for Company Commanders but sometimes used for the Officer Leader at any level) has all the answers. After spending the day talking to my soldiers and trying to meld with my Platoon Sergeant I was ready for some relaxation. We had free steaks at the Officer's Club and I washed my meal down with several Scotches.

20 November: I received word that I was assigned as the Investigating Officer on an Accident Investigation Board. It was deemed as a minor accident so I was the only one on the board.

21 November: I made the trek across the airfield to inspect the aircraft that was involved in the accident. It seems that a CAV pilot had flown his AH-1G Huey Cobra under a bridge. He almost made it without incident but his tail rotor clipped the bridge as he was pulling pitch to climb out on the other side. He was fortunate to have escaped with minor damage to the tail rotor and stabilizer (the airfoil near the end of the tail boom that provides stability in flight). While I was gone, Marshall Eubanks got word that he was leaving three days early and had to leave in a rush. Marshall was a good friend to me who took me in confidence early on after my arrival and showed me "the ropes".

22 November: I was able to write up the accident in such a manner that it was reduced to an incident which spared the CAV pilot further embarrassment and probably saved his career. Later that evening, Ayers, Parker, Knight, and I had several Scotches at the O Club in honor of Marshall's DEROS (Date of Expected Return from Overseas).

23 November: We had our Thanksgiving dinner in the mess hall today; I dined with Ayers and Parker. It was a slow day; Flight OPS scheduled only essential missions so most everyone had a day off. I laid around the hooch most of the day, watched NFL Films in the O Club, wrote Gerann, and hit the rack around 2300 hours.

24 November: I finally finished all the paperwork required for the investigation and put a lid on it around 1530 hours. My energy level was at about zero so I went to the O Club, watched NFL Films for a while, then went to my hooch and hit the rack around 2300 hours after writing Gerann. P.S. I was informed today that my DFC (Distinguished Flying Cross) was downgraded to an Air Medal with a "V" for valor.

25 November: I finally got back to my platoon today. It was a slow day being Saturday (Flight Operations tried to schedule missions light on weekends). We didn't have too many "Birds" (Helicopters) going out today.

We had free steaks tonight at the O Club with a band (same one that was there on my first night in Can Tho). The beer was flowing freely and after a while the CAV (Air Cavalry) pilots and the CAC (Corps Aviation Company) pilots started yelling at one another. We were just blowing off steam so after a while it subsided and we all went to our hooch's and crashed for the evening.

27 November: Tom Arnold called from Saigon today around 0900 hours. He's doing fine, flying "Snakes" (AH-1G Cobra) with a CAV unit out of Ben Hoa near Saigon. I worked with one of my mainte-nance teams 'til 1830 hours; we had several "No Go's" from a test flight to correct. We finally got the Bird to MC (Mission Capable). I ate a late supper in the O Club and crashed (went to bed) early.

28 November: I called Beetle (David Bailey) today; he may come down for a visit soon.

2 December: Dale Wells got in country a few days ago and arrived today in Can Tho; he's going to be in my platoon as one of my test pilots since he just came from AMOC (Aircraft Maintenance Officer Course). We met Dale and Nancy Wells at Fort Wolters. He was a couple of classes behind me and they lived right next to us in the same duplex at 305 NW 25th Street. Later Dale caught up with me at Fort Eustis while I was attending AMOC. Again, he was a couple of classes behind me. They had a cute little blond headed boy name Ty. *About three years later, Gerann and I would meet Tim and Caren Reed in Rutledge, Georgia and they too had a cute little blond headed boy named Ty! Tragically we lost Ty Reed in an automobile accident just a few weeks before his high school grad-uation in 1993. We founded the Ty Reed Golf Classic in 2009 to raise money for the scholarship fund in memory of Ty. Since 1993, there have been eighty five scholarships awarded in memory of Ty.* All missions were cancelled today because of a typhoon warning. I thought man, this weather here is really crazy!

4 December: I finally had my check ride today with the Unit IP (In-structor Pilot); no problems, it went just about perfectly. This was a for-mality that had to be accomplished before I could perform test flights.

6 December: We had a recovery mission to An Toi Island today. The Navy had a base there and on a resupply mission one of our Birds broke. We fixed the broke Bird and then went swimming and skiing in the South China Sea. The Navy boys had fashioned some homemade skis from scrap lumber. Never thought I'd be slalom skiing in the Gulf of Thailand next to the South China Sea, we had a blast.

7 December: Ouch! Nobody will ever believe I got sun burned in Vietnam while water skiing in the South China Sea in December.

8 December: Worked late today; we had trouble getting tail number 811 up. Finally at 2045, I was able to sign off and declare it "MC" (Mission Capable). I called "Beetle" today but he wasn't in his office. I was told he was on the golf course. I thought, wow, war in MACV Headquarters must be tough.

As we neared Christmas, things began to slow down. The peace talks in Paris were still going on. It seemed that the VC and NVA were anticipating that an agreement might be reached soon and they didn't want to do anything drastic to delay it. With the reduction in missions also came a lighter workload for my Maintenance Platoon. Consequently, we spent many hours in the Officer's Club having a 'few' beers, shooting pool, and playing ping pong.

We still had our practice alerts periodically. A loud siren would sound and everybody would come rushing out of their 'hooch' with their steel pots on their heads and their assigned weapon in hand. We would sit there in the bunker until another siren sounded all clear.

16 December: Our 'Super Shaft' patches were finished today! Heretofore, the call sign of the maintenance platoon had been 'Short Shaft'. The name was coined because the shaft that connected the transmission to the main rotor was the short shaft. I always thought the name was somewhat demeaning. When the UH-1H Model was introduced, the short shaft beefed up and was renamed super shaft. Since we had a fleet of H Models (we did have three or four D Models) I felt it was time for a change in our call sign to "Super Shaft". We used the logo of Arm and Hammer Baking Soda and had the hand holding, what else, a Super Shaft. We added some lightning bolts to jazz it up a bit and the platoon patch was worn on the right shirt pocket. It really looked cool and from then on, our call sign was 'Super Shaft'; being the platoon leader, I was 'Super Shaft' six.

17 December: We had a Christmas Party downtown at Harry's house (I don't remember who Harry was or why he was living downtown?) One incident in my notes recounted an accident of a little Vietnamese girl that was hit by a ¾ ton truck. Earl Shaw and I took her to the dispensary and fortunately she checked out with no significant injuries.

22 December: I received a Christmas Card from Eubanks today! I thought, man it must be great to be home for Christmas.

23 December: I talked to Beetle today; he's going to see Bob Hope. I guess that's one of the perks of being in Saigon.

24 December: I finally talked to Gary King today. We talked on the phone for about an hour. He's doing OK but like all of us really missing home, especially at Christmas.

25 December: There was a long line early at the Tiki Hut. MARS (Military Auxiliary Radio System) was located there and being Christmas Day everybody wanted to call home. I got through to our number but Gerann wasn't at home. Because of the International Date Line, it was actually 24 December back home so I'm not sure why she wasn't at home.

27 December: We had a recovery mission to Tra Vinh today. Tail number 314 went down with a Tail Rotor Chip Light. Dale went with me; I flew the 'sick bird' back and Dale trailed me in the other ship. As a maintenance test pilot, we often had to fly with caution lights and strange noises. If a 'broke ship' was flyable at all, we would bring it back rather than work on it in the field.

29 December: Another late night in the maintenance platoon; we had picked up a 'broke bird' from the 611th and after repeated attempts to get her up we finally succeeded. I talked to David Bailey (Beetle) today; we talked frequently until his DEROS. He left for 'The World' just a few weeks before I did.

30 December: Went downtown with CPT Zec to get our seats in the platoon jeep covered. We also had a custom made spare tire cover made with our platoon Super Shaft Logo; it looks cool. CPT Zec was just 'marking time' until his DEROS (Date Expected Return from Overseas) since I had already taken over the maintenance platoon. I called Gerann from the hanger (the MARS folks patched me through their system) but she wasn't home.

31 December: New Year's Eve in Vietnam was a pretty uneventful day. I had breakfast at the Officer's Club with Dale and afterwards we shot a couple games of pool. I tried to call Gerann in the afternoon but she was at Mountain Park. We had a band at the Club that evening; everybody got drunk, there was dancing on the tables, etc. I guess we were all trying to drown our sorrows because at this point the War was more of a nuisance than anything. We all were ready to get home and get on with the rest of our lives. Little did we know that very soon things would begin to move rapidly and we would all be home within 90 days.

1 January 1973: I took the morning off; called Gerann but she was gone.

2 January: I talked to Gerann today; we are planning to take R & R (Rest and Relaxation) in Hawaii beginning 1 April. Of course, I didn't know at the time that I would be home by then. Shortly after that we received word that all R & R leaves would be denied.

4 January: The 164th CAG (Combat Aviation Group) was activated 20 December 1967 at Can Tho with two CABs (Combat Aviation Battalion), the 13th CAB and the 307th CAB and a total of nine Aviation Companies. In September of 1971, the 164th was reorganized to include a third CAB, the 214th, and the 7/1 ACS (Armored Cavalry Squadron) and a total of 12 Aviation Companies, five ACTs (Armored Cavalry Troop) and one Artillery Unit, H/29 ARTY. There was another reorganization in January 1972; the 164th was reduced to the 13th CAB with four subordinate units and the 7/1 ACS with four subordinate units. The 18th CAC (Corps Aviation Company) was not included. The 18th CAC was "stood up" again on 1 June 1971 and remained part of the 164th CAG until it's deactivation at the end of the war. In September of 1972, the 164th was reorganized one final time with just three subordinate units, 18th CAC, C/16 ACT and 611th TC (Transportation Company).

We received a recovery mission on the morning of 4 January 1973. C/16 had a "slick" (UH-1H) down near Moc Hoa with a blade separation. This basically meant that one of the two main rotor blades was coming apart. Obviously, this was a dangerous situation and the pilots who successfully landed the "bird" did a remarkable job since the vibration would have been tremendous. Moc Hoa was in the Long An Province near the Cambodian border. Dale Wells flew with me as my "Peter Pilot" (second in command) and me as the PIC (Pilot in Command). Visibility was poor, maybe about ½ to ¾ mile, low ceiling and drizzling rain; a lovely day for a recovery mission. We arrived on station in about 30 minutes (it was a short flight from Can Tho). We had to sling load the downed "bird" under a Chinook (CH-47). The trick to sling loading is to adjust the straps so the "bird" being hauled is in a slightly nose down attitude. If this is not the case, then the belly of the aircraft being recovered will be exposed to the airstream created by the forward movement and will become unstable. This could cause loss of the aircraft being recovered if the Chinook pilot has to "punch" the load off (in other words drop it). Dale and I flew escort for the Chinook and observed the load for any possible problems. Fortunately, my crew did a great job and we returned to Can Tho with the sick "bird" in tow safely.

6 January: Ever since I've been in Vietnam, our Officer's Club had free steaks and nickel beer on Saturday or Sunday. Well, today the steaks weren't free; they cost fifty cents!

Dale Wells was my assistant Platoon Leader; he and I spent a great deal of time together the last three months before our DEROS. As I stated before, Dale and I had met at Fort Wolters while we were both attending Primary Helicopter Training; Dale was a couple of classes behind me, thus he didn't arrive in country until early December. The two of us spent our idle time shooting pool and playing ping pong in the "O Club" and we ate many meals together. Dale was a strong Christian. Thinking back, I believe he had a good influence on me even though in that day I didn't want to hear anything about The Bible or God. Thankfully, a few years later, I was saved shortly after the birth of our oldest son Chris.

In those last days, we began transferring all the "Hueys" into the 18th CAC. One by one we picked up everything that C/16 ACT and 611th TC (Transportation Company) had. Our inventory went from 20 Hueys to 34! It was my task as the Aircraft Maintenance Officer to insure that each one would be in a mission capable (MC) condition when the time came to transfer them to the VNAF (Vietnamese Air Force). My forty-man Maintenance Platoon was shrinking fast because we were shipping soldiers home every day.

14 January: Got up at 0700 hours. I talked flight operations into scheduling a mission to Vung Tau. This was the in-country R & R Center located on the coast of the South China Sea. Dale and I took a couple of soldiers with us. We spent the day swimming, playing basketball, ping pong, putt-putt golf, and generally just enjoying being at the beach. They even had a batting cage so we tried our hand at hitting a few fastballs. It was a welcomed relief from the boredom of being in Can Tho with very little to do in the way of missions. We had plenty to do regarding getting ready to turn over the compound and equipment to the VNAF but none of us were very enthused about that mission. As it turned out, this was the last time I'd have an opportunity to relax for an entire day. Things were going to pick up fast. We flew back later that evening; Dale and I went to downtown Can Tho to shop for souvenirs.

15 January: I called Beetle (David Bailey) today; he told me that Miami had won Super Bowl VII over Washington, completing the first perfect season (17-0) in the history of the NFL!

19 January: We worked 'til 2000 hours today on tail number 709. We got a CW3 in today with two previous tours under his belt. I heard the "old man" (Company Commander) was going to put him in my platoon as a test pilot; I can use the help.

21 January: We worked 'til 2230 hours today fixing a tail rotor failure. The pilot had to land in a local soccer field. I was beat so I just opened a can of tuna in the room and then crashed in my bunk.

22 January: Earle drove me to the soccer field and I flew tail number 716 back to the airfield. It was a short flight which was good because I had several caution lights.

24 January: The long-awaited Peace Agreement was announced by "Tricky Dick" (President Nixon) today.

The United States, South Vietnam, Viet Cong, and North Vietnam formally signed "An Agreement Ending the War and Restoring Peace in Vietnam". This was accomplished at the peace talks in Paris. Due to South Vietnam's unwillingness to recognize the Viet Cong's Provisional Revolutionary Government, all references to it were confined to a two-party version of the document signed by North Vietnam and the United States—the South Vietnamese were presented with a separate document that did not make reference to the Viet Cong government. This was part of Saigon's long-time refusal to recognize the Viet Cong as a legitimate participant in the discussions to end the war.

The settlement included a cease-fire throughout Vietnam. In addition, the United States agreed to the withdrawal of all U.S. troops and advisors (totaling about 23,700) and the dismantling of all U.S. bases within 60 days. In return, the North Vietnamese agreed to release all U.S. and other prisoners of war.

Both sides agreed to the withdrawal of all foreign troops from Laos and Cambodia and the prohibition of bases in and troop movements through those countries. It was agreed that the DMZ at the 17th Parallel would remain a provisional dividing line, with eventual reunification of the country "through peaceful means." An international control commission would be established made up of Canadians, Hungarians, Poles, and Indonesians, with 1,160 inspectors to supervise the agreement. According to the agreement, South Vietnamese President Nguyen Van Thieu would continue in office pending elections. Agreeing to "the South Vietnamese People's right to self-determination," the North Vietnamese said they would not initiate military movement across the DMZ and that there would be no use of force to reunify the country. Of course, a little more than two years later they broke the terms of the peace agreement when the NVA mounted a massive military operation against the south and overran Saigon. More on this under 25 January.

25 January: Up at 0530, meetings all morning. It's official, we're getting the CAV's Hueys.

Under the provision of the Peace Agreement, there will be a four-nation group to oversee our withdrawal. Canada, Indonesia, Hungary, and Poland are the four nations. For the next few weeks, we averaged 12-14 hour days. We had to paint orange strips around the tail boom of each Huey (we called these "Zebra Birds") and then on some selected ones we had to Stencil in large letters ICCS (International Commission for Control and Supervision). Later, it was decided there should be a bright magenta green around the letters. (see 1 March note) That made a really great target!

Below comments were copied from the following website: http://www.americanforeignrelations.com/O-W/The-Vietnam-War-and-Its-Impact-The-peace-agreement.html

An International Commission of Control and Supervision (ICCS), consisting of Canada, Hungary, Indonesia, and Poland, would oversee the agreement and report violations. In No Peace, No Honor (2001), Larry Berman utilized recently declassified records to show that Nixon had little faith in the Paris accord and expected that the accord would be violated, which would trigger a brutal military response.

Not a moment of peace ever came to Vietnam. Following the return of the American POWs, there was little adherence to the Paris agreements from either North or South Vietnam. The U.S. troops departed Vietnam

sixty days after the Paris agreement was signed, but the level of violence had not significantly declined. Watergate was about to destroy the Nixon presidency and a new antiwar Congress had little interest in continuing economic support to the South.

Indeed, a little more than two years after our withdrawal, the NVA and VC overran Saigon and toppled the government of what was left of a free South Vietnam. All the while our U.S. Congress "sat on their hands" and refused to send even one dollar of aid to our allies that we had fought so gallantly for to insure their freedom. It was a tragic end to a war that had cost us over 58,000 lives of brave Americans and billions of dollars in aid and equipment. In fact, some of the thirty-four UH-1H Helicopters that I had signed over to the VNAF in March of 1973 were purposely crashed into the South China Sea by VNAF pilots. They were desperately hoping to escape a brutal fate that would await them at the hands of a communist government. They would swim to our ships that were anchored off the coast, knowing that our sailors would pull them to safety. Some of those helicopters that weren't crashed into the sea are now serving as "make shift" homes for impoverished Vietnamese Families who have suffered horribly under the oppressive communist regime.

28 January: We worked late last night and woke up this morning to incoming 122mm rounds! One of our "Zebra Birds" got shot up southwest of Can Tho. "Peter Pilot" WO1 Anthony Dal Poza took a round through his head and was killed instantly. He had been in country just a few weeks. Also, a US Colonel took a round through his leg. I thought, man, this peace treaty is really not working. Dale Wells and I attended a memorial service at the base of the tower.

From a retired officer who was a passenger on Mr. Dal Pozzo's flight. K. Kobata

> "Landing in Chuong Thien to pick up one more passenger, Mr. Dal Pozzo expertly flew us rather low, directly following a large canal north to Can Tho. About ten minutes into the flight, we approached a very large rice mill and waving on a pole was the largest Viet Cong flag I have ever seen. From nowhere appeared a single VC aiming and firing an AK-47 automatic weapon at the Huey. I heard the snap-snap-snap of the bullets hitting the Huey, and I saw bullet holes appearing on the aluminum floor by my feet. Mr. Dal Pozzo was struck on his helmet and slumped over. The soldier sitting directly in front of me winced and screamed, "I'm hit!!" and I saw blood staining his trousers. Worrying about myself, I quickly examined my feet and legs, and I was OK. Sitting on the left side I saw the green rice paddy quickly approaching me. Mr. Dal Pozzo was hit fatally and released the controls and the Huey was going to crash. Suddenly Mr. Goodheart grabbed the controls and regained altitude after quite a bit of yawing and shuddering. For years I tried to remember your name, Mr. Dal Pozzo. I could not. I visited the travelling "Vietnam Veterans Memorial Wall" twice to search for your name on the right (war ending) side of the wall. I looked at the Wall Book and searched for your name but could not remember it. I wanted to honor you for what you did and for your service. You are a true hero and your family and loved ones can forever be proud of you. I will always remember you and your smiling handsome face. God Bless you!"

The following account is from Colonel (Retired) Jerry Childers who was our Company Commander.

> Sadly I remember it well. I helped take him out of the aircraft. I pulled his helmet off and was astonished to see that round barely got inside his

132

head. His door gunners only had pistols due to first day of cease fire and rule that they were restricted to "personal side arms". The next day I designated fully automatic M16s as personal side arms. We flew with them until stand down without a problem and no further losses.

28 January: To add fuel to the fire, MAJ Runk was complaining about having only eight of 18 "Birds" flyable. My forty-man platoon was down to about 20 which included four pilots, platoon sergeant, three inspectors, and just 12 mechanics. We were doing the best we could with limited personnel and resources. Because of the slow down, repair parts were coming slowly.

30 January: I talked to "Beetle" today; he's going home at X + 45 too.

1 February: Things are looking better; we got four more aircraft up (MC) today.

6 February: Talked to G-1 in Saigon about my next assignment. I'm going to PCS (Permanent Change of Station) back to Fort Eustis. Dale is going to Fort Lewis, Washington.

As time went along we all played a lot of games to pass the time, i.e. horseshoes, pool, ping pong, basketball, etc. We did everything possible to stay busy with work of course and then when we had time off, in order to fight boredom we busied ourselves with anything to help pass the time.

8 February: I called Gary King and David Bailey today. They're both getting restless just like all of us. Bill Bryan, one of my 71-44 flight classmates, dropped by my hanger today. He was on his way to Saigon and they stopped in for fuel and lunch. We reminisced about flight school and shared a few war stories before he left. I talked to Gerann.

The connection was great; she and Judy are moving out of the house before we get back.

11 February: I shot a couple games of pool with the Canadians and Poles at the Officer's Club. I woke up at 2AM to a strange noise. I had a rat loose in my room! Rather than fight him, I took my mattress to Dale's room and crashed in there.

12 February: We had our Awards & Decorations Ceremony today. I received a Bronze Star for Meritorious Service and an Air Medal with "V" Device for Valor. This was for the mission in Cambodia when we called in air strikes on a Khmer Rouge Position. The Captain I flew with and I were both recommended for a DFC (Distinguished Flying Cross). Mine was downgraded to the Air Medal with "V"; this was a common practice during Vietnam that lower ranking personnel did not usually get the same recognition as their superiors, even though the risk, etc. may have been commensurate. Oh well, all these years later, I'm thankful that The Lord protected me from injury and that I was able to perform under pressure. Also, I received six Air Medals (one for each 50 hours of combat support missions).

After the ceremony, there was a cookout in the hanger and we all kicked back and relaxed, all the while thinking about home.

14 February: MAJ Runk was excited about us getting tail number 811 up. However, the excitement was short lived when Dale found excessive play in the Gimbal Ring Bearing (this was in the Swashplate which controls the pitch of the rotor blades) and a crack in one of the main rotor blades.

15 February: I was briefed today that my Maintenance Platoon officially stands down on 28 February. There will be a special POW Team and I will be on it with my Maintenance Crew (seven people, i.e. two pilots, two inspectors, platoon sergeant, and three mechanics). My thoughts were mixed; certainly a noble mission but at the same time it may delay my return home.

16 February: There was a Chinook (CH-47) shot down near An Loc today. Both pilots survived, along with three passengers, but all sustained injuries. Man, this peace agreement is killing us! Had a few scotches in the club with my Platoon Sergeant Faustich and a few others, Parker, Tyler, and Hyatt.

17 February: VNAF Team came by today and looked at all the tool sets, etc. that we'll be turning over to them shortly. I didn't like their smug attitude. You'd think they'd be overjoyed considering all the sacrifice we've made for them for so long.

18 February: Had coffee in Tiki Hut with Tyler. I played horseshoes and basketball at the hanger until noon then to the club for lunch. I met some of our NCOs at Candy's Country Music downtown for supper and drinks.

19: February: The VNAF Team didn't show today. They were supposed to sign for a bunch of equipment. SFC Faustich and I beat everyone in horseshoes.

20 February: I called 'Beetle' today; he's leaving on 4 March. We loaded all our excess equipment onto flatbeds and will send it with George to Saigon tomorrow. There's no telling what may eventually happen to all that stuff.

21 February: VNAF showed today; they signed for all the tool sets, kits, and outfits that were part of the stuff for the CH-47s. Dale, George, and I met some of the NCOs downtown for a few beers in the afternoon. Once back to the hanger, Dale and I won the horseshoe tournament. We're desperate for something to keep the boredom from overtaking us.

22 February: I went downtown to look for a souvenir for Gerann, to no avail.

24 February: Movie in the club was *The Graduate;* George and I sat around talking until 2300 hours. Bored!

25 February: This was typical of our 'last days'. Breakfast at the club, horseshoes, ping-pong, and strip show back at the club; thinking back now you can see more at the beach today. That afternoon Lee, SFC Hyatt, and I went to Candy's Bar downtown for drinks and Country Music. All the Vietnamese bands of that day were well versed in the most popular American Music, especially current Rock & Roll and Country.

27 February: Dale and I moved out of our rooms into the 'Hillclimber Lounge'. We had already started turning over various buildings to the ARVN (Army of Vietnam) and the VNAF so we had to vacate our sleeping quarters. We also shipped our hold baggage today so we're getting closer to actually leaving.

1 March: We had to repaint all the ICCS 'Birds' today. They decided the letters ICCS weren't visible enough. We painted a magenta green around all the block letters. That really made a bright target. George and I spent the afternoon at the club attempting to drown our boredom in several scotches. George and I got to be close friends the last couple of months. He like Dale was a late arrival and since he was AMOC qualified the Old Man assigned him to my platoon as a test

pilot. He was a good officer. Unfortunately, like so many others, I've never seen or heard from him since we left Vietnam.

2 March: We moved the Maintenance Office today. I talked to the Old Man about MAJ Runk; he's the Commander of the 611th and he keeps getting into my business. MAJ Childers, my Commander, said he'd take care of it. Jerry Childers was a great commander. He gave his leaders the support and encouragement they needed to perform at the highest level and he always defended his soldiers. SSG Lismore and I went to Binh Thuy to get an oil line for tail #146. Binh Thuy was an airbase located just 7km Northwest of Can Tho. It was constructed by our Army Engineers in 1965 and was in use throughout the war by US Navy, US Air Force, and VNAF. I believe we probably went to either LSI (Lear Siegler International) or Air America. We always had a good relationship with all our American contractors; we helped each other with parts and advice on an ongoing basis, especially in these last days as our supply lines were beginning to dry up.

3 March: The Maintenance Platoon went to a floating restaurant in downtown Can Tho for a farewell party of sorts. We then all went to a couple of bars and had a few drinks. Things are really starting to get loose.

4 March: I called "Beetle" at 0300 hours; he's leaving for "the world" today. We had to ship 17 people today with just four hours notice. Things are moving fast but I'm still here.

5 March: I'm down to just eight soldiers, Dale and me as Pilots, SFC Faust as Platoon Sergeant, two Inspectors, and three mechanics.

6 March: The VNAF signed for some more stuff today. We painted six more ICCS Birds. We watched the "Last Picture Show" at the Club (the Enlisted & Officer's Club was now combined because of low numbers) and as it turned out it was the last movie we'd see in Vietnam and it was the first movie I saw in Vietnam back when I just arrived in country and stayed with Beetle in Saigon.

9 March: Up early to Saigon. We turned in six "Birds" to the ICCS today; all were ICCS Birds. Saw Bill Bryan (he was in my Flight Class 71-44) and Barry Miller. We all went to the Officer's Club and talked for hours.

The next several days were filled with whatever we could think of to keep our minds off going home; we spent time at our meager swimming pool on the compound, pitched horseshoes next to the hangar, shot pool in the O. Club, watched movies, and wrote home.

12 March: Dale and I flew to Saigon to get our finance records. We had lunch at the O. Club on Ton Son Knut Airbase and saw Jay Hamilton at Flight Operations.

15 March: Entry in my calendar today was BOREDOM BAD!

16 March: Had breakfast with my Platoon Sergeant, SFC Faustich, and SP4 Merrow. Merrow was a good ole South Georgia boy and one of the best aircraft mechanics I've ever known. Later that night SFC Faustich and I had a good long conversation; we really had a good working relationship and his mentorship helped me throughout my entire career.

19 March: Wow, don't feel too good today after indulging in one too many last night at the O. Club. Dale and I flew tail number 146 today, all systems go so it's MC (Mission Capable). Boredom is getting bad; everybody wants to go home!

21 March: Dale and I flew 727 and 755 today, all good, MC. I called Gary King and he's in the same boat as me, just marking time and waiting.

23 March: BOREDOM!

24 March: Transferred tail number 145 to the VNAF today. We had a floor show in the O. Club complete with stripper, bad!

26 March: There was much excitement among the locals today because South Vietnamese President Thieu was scheduled to be in Can Tho. We're scheduled to transfer all remaining "birds" to the VNAF tomorrow.

27 March: Got up at 0630. I met the VNAF team in my hangar after breakfast. I had my entire team there (me, Dale, Faustich, Merrow, one warrant, and two inspectors). They showed up with their inspection team and after spending about 30 minutes on the first helicopter they handed me a "gig" sheet with numerous write-ups. The VNAF Captain said, "You fix." I took the sheet, glanced at it, handed it back to him and said, "You want, you sign!" This was the same drill we'd gone through before when turning over aircraft to them and each time it was the same, they signed. They signed for all remaining UH-1H Hueys (28 I believe). As I left the maintenance hangar for the last time, I reached up and turned off the lights. It seemed like a good thing to do to close out this chapter of my life and of our American military's experience in Vietnam.

We left Can Tho at 1250 on a C-130 bound for Saigon. At Camp Alpha on Ton Son Knut I saw John Hirsch, Jay Hamilton, Jesse Blanco, Bill Bryan, Gary King, and many others. It was a festive occasion; we all went to the Officer's Club for supper and drinks. The food was decent and band, "The Dreamers", was OK. We'll be heading home tomorrow!

28 March: Got up at 0620. Mike, Dale, Gary, and I had breakfast in the Mess Hall. Afterwards we all went to a "Dink" Shop and bought ribbons and a few other souvenirs. We all loaded onto a big beautiful orange Boeing 747 Jumbo Jet (first one I ever saw). One of the few downers was the NVA and VC troops observing the withdrawal. It was surreal. Just a few days earlier they were our enemies and now they were standing among us. At 1800 hours, the pilot of the big jet taxied onto the runway, backed up so as to hang the plane's tail over the end of the runway, and started to do his run-up procedure. At 1814, we started rolling down the runway and after utilizing every inch of available runway we lifted off at 1815 hours! Shouts and cheers were deafening!!

I I. BACK IN THE WORLD, HOME SWEET HOME

28 March 1973: We made two stops; one in Guam and the other in Hawaii before landing in San Francisco at 2215 hours on 28 March!

28 March: We touched down at San Francisco Airport at 2215 hours; wow, it felt good to be back in "the World"! When you travel from west to east and cross the international dateline you subtract a day. Essentially, we arrived in SF the same day we left Saigon but just about four hours later. Actual travel time was about 28 hours counting our stops in Guam and Hawaii. I purchased my ticket to Atlanta and called Gerann.

29 March: We touched down at the Atlanta Airport at 0920 hours. Gerann was there to meet me and we headed to Royal Coach Motor Inn where we had spent our first honeymoon night. They weren't going to have our room ready until 1200 so we jumped in the car and went across the bridge to the Mark Inn. Home Sweet Home, it's good to be back with Gerann.

30 March: Jet lag is real, but I didn't care; I was home! Gerann and I

141

got up early and went to the little restaurant on the edge of Georgia Tech's campus where her Aunt Kathryn worked. We had a great breakfast and got to visit with Kathryn. We took Kathryn and Melvin's son Marty to get his driver's license in Marietta but they weren't open so we instead took him to Confederate Avenue. Little did I know that 30 years later (2003-2008), I would have an office "on the hill" behind the State Patrol Headquarters and would serve as the Surface Maintenance Manager (SMM) for the Georgia Army National Guard. That afternoon Gerann and I went to Mother and Daddy's new home in Milner, Georgia for dinner (by the way dinner is the middle meal of the day; supper is the last meal of the day). Gerann did a fantastic job in getting them moved out of Atlanta while I was away. Their new place was a "Jim Walters" home, three bedrooms and one bath on about a half-acre lot out in the country. In fact, it was on a dirt road in Lamar County, perfect place for them. Mother and Daddy both seemed to really appreciate having a nice place in the country and I was so pleased that we had them out of Atlanta and the old neighborhood which was going "downhill" fast. After a great visit, we headed back to our "headquarters", Kathryn and Melvin's house. Melvin and I went to a pool hall on Marietta Street and shot a few games of pool. Melvin was prone to drink to excess on occasion but we just had a couple of beers and enjoyed each other's company; I always liked Melvin and we got along together great over the years. Some years later, he and Kathryn moved to Florida and we didn't get to see them very often; I have many fond memories of spending time at their little house in Atlanta which we used as our "headquarters" when we'd come to Atlanta during my Active Duty years (1970-1974).

31 March: We go up early and went to the Post Exchange (PX) at Fort McPherson to do a little shopping. We happened to see Mike and Lynn Carden there. As I recall, Mike had also been in Vietnam but he wasn't an Aviator. Being a Transportation Officer, he and Lynn would be stationed back at Fort Eustis along with us, Tom and Vickie Arnold, John and Cheryl Hirsch, Gary and Judy King, and several others. We had some great times there as young married folks just enjoying life and really not thinking much about the future. After our shopping excursion at the PX, we headed to Mountain Park for lunch with Gerann's parents, Red and Florence. They were always great and were more like another set of parents rather than in-laws. We had a great visit with them and then onto Joan and Clyde's for supper. My sister and brother-in-law were special as well. Through the years, we did a lot with them and they always visited us when we were moving around during our active duty time as did Red and Florence. Later that evening, we decided to check into the Mark Inn near Six Flags over Georgia for some badly needed rest and relaxation.

1 April: We slept late then went to Ma Maw and Pa Paw's for Sunday dinner. The whole McElreath and Smith clans were there. It was good to see everybody. Late that afternoon we headed back to Mableton to Joan and Clyde's for supper. Mother, Daddy, and Brother Harold were there as well. Harold "drilled" me with numerous questions about my experiences in Vietnam. He was my older brother (by eight years) but he always "looked up" to me and was one of my greatest encouragers. I phoned my nephew Jeff who was, I believe, in Texas at Abilene Christian College and after a great day of reconnecting with family, Gerann and I arrived back at our "headquarters", Kathryn and Melvin's house.

2-5 April: The next four days we spent doing some shopping, more visiting of family and generally just getting readjusted to being back in "the world". We made another trip to Mother and Daddy's, had a meal with Sharon and Larry (Gerann's sister and brother-in-law) and made a trip to Monroe and had supper with Cecil, Ellen (my oldest brother and sister-in-law), and their family.

6 April: We pulled out early for Oklahoma to visit my brother Robert and his family. After about twelve hours on the road we stopped for the night in Fort Smith, Arkansas. One of my favorite places to eat back then was Bonanza Steak House and that's where we enjoyed a great meal that evening.

7 April: We arrived at Robert and Inez's house around noon. It was great to see them and all the kids, Bob, Randell, and Robyn. Robert had a new Buick with all the "bells and whistles" of the day. We decided to eat supper at a local steak house, Glenn's. As the four of us were walking away from the car, the headlights were still on because the automatic shut-off had not yet engaged. A little boy on the sidewalk, probably about twelve or thirteen years old, called out to my brother, "Hey Mister, you left your lights on!" Without hesitating Robert turned back toward the car and in an exaggerated motion pretended to "blow out the headlights". At that same moment, the automatic shut-off did its job and the lights went out as if Robert had magically blown them out. Well, that little boy's eyes doubled in size and he looked at my brother with the most whimsical look you could imagine. We all had a good laugh about that as we continued toward the door. Over the years, we've laughed about that numerous times and by the way, we enjoyed a great steak that made Bonanza look like "Minor League".

8-15 April: During the next several days we packed in a lot of visiting, eating, shopping, sightseeing, and just great quality time with Robert and his Family.

Dale and Linda Wells came in on 12 April and stayed one night. Dale had been my Assistant Platoon Leader in Vietnam and we had known one another before that at Fort Eustis and throughout Flight School, even though we weren't in the same Flight Class. Dale, Linda, Gerann, and I went to the Cowboy Hall of Fame. They had a little blonde headed boy named Ty who was maybe around four or five years old at that time. It's sort of ironic that just a couple of years later we would become close friends with Tim and Caren Reed who also had a little blonde headed boy named Ty. (I referred to this briefly in an earlier part of this story but here's more detail) Ty Reed would later meet an untimely death in March of 1993 just a few weeks before his high school graduation at Morgan County High School. Tim and Caren established the "Ty Reed Memorial Scholarship" Inc. and have awarded eighty five scholarships to graduating seniors in memory of Ty since then. In 2009, we started the "Ty Reed Golf Classic" to raise money for the scholarship fund and as of this writing we have raised $106,000 with eleven tournaments. We give all the glory to our Lord and Savior Jesus Christ!

Jeff Carson, my nephew, arrived on 13 April (he was in school at Abilene Christian College, ACC). Jeff, Robert, Inez, Gerann, and I stayed up late just talking, laughing, and having a great time. Jeff stayed a couple of nights and on Sunday, 15 April he headed back to ACC and Gerann and I left for Georgia.

We spent the night in Savannah, Tennessee at Long's Motel. Back in that day there were still a number of locally owned motels and many of them were a good bargain and well maintained.

16 April: We made our way back to "headquarters", Kathryn and Melvin's house, after stopping at "Natural Bridge" which was a huge disappointment.

17 April: Heading back to Fort Eustis tomorrow so we made a whirlwind tour. We started with breakfast at Kathryn's restaurant (she

145

worked at a little café just off the Georgia Tech Campus and we referred to it as her restaurant). Then we went by Ma Maw and Pa Paw's, Fort Mac PX, Mother and Daddy's for a big dinner, Joan and Clyde's for supper, Mountain Park for a late visit, and finally back to "headquarters".

18 April: Pulled out at 10:30 after breakfast at Kathryn's restaurant. We arrived in Newport News at 8PM and spent the night at the Econo Travel Inn on Jefferson Boulevard.

19-25 April: The next few days were spent taking care of business with various offices on post such as Finance, Personnel, Medical, Aviation, etc. and looking for a place to live. We signed up for on post housing but there was a waiting list. We spent time with Gary and Judy King, Tom and Vickie Arnold, and others.

25 April: Rented a two-bedroom town house at Court House Green.

Over the next several days I spent time going to Personnel to see about my next job and shopping for furniture for our new place. We bought $1,200 worth of furniture at Sears. We took the money we had saved for R & R in Hawaii and put it on the furniture.

2 May: I'm the Executive Officer of the 155th Terminal Service Company. The Commander is CPT Wiebe, an odd sort of fellow. I served for several months in that capacity. During that time, many of our soldiers were malcontents (draftees were not always "happy" to be in the Army) and caused a number of discipline problems; my patience and tact was tried on numerous occasions as I administered the code of military justice. I regularly handed out Article 15s. The result was usually a reduction in rank and/or withholding a designated amount of money from their next paycheck. The duty wasn't very enjoyable but looking back I gained some valuable experience that would benefit me years later in my military career.

24-31 May: Tom Arnold had a great job at the airfield, working in maintenance. He told me about an opening in the 214th Medical Detachment. I interviewed with the commander of the unit. They were looking for a pilot with "boo coos" of flying hours so I had no chance at that position.

1 June: I called my first ball game with the Athletic Officials Association (AOA) today, a girls' softball contest. Monk Mayhue got me involved in this. Tom Arnold also was a member. We called softball (both slow pitch and fast pitch), Little League Baseball, Service League Baseball (those guys could really play!), football and basketball.

During basketball season, I was on my way to the Naval Weapons Station in Yorktown to call a game on base. I was running late so I was exceeding the posted speed limit (45 mph in a 25 mph zone). Of course, a local cop pulled me over and asked for driver's license, registration, insurance etc. I was driving our new Oldsmobile Cutlass Sport which had an Alabama tag. We had bought it in Enterprise, Alabama when I was at Fort Rucker in Flight School so we just kept the Alabama registration since we were moving so often. Alabama didn't require a vehicle safety inspection but Virginia did, so we had a Virginia Inspection Sticker. Being from Georgia, of course I had a Georgia Driver's License. Proof of Automobile Insurance was required so I flashed my USAA Insurance card which had a Texas address since the company's home office is in San Antonio. When I began explaining the combination of Alabama, Virginia, Georgia, and Texas connections, it was just too much for the policeman to comprehend and in disgust he said, "Just go, but please slow down!"

During the rest of 1973 and until I left active duty in August of

147

1974, Gerann and I enjoyed the "good life" of being married, having many friends, and really not considering the future. We spent much quality time with our friends. There was bowling, golf, movies, concerts, dances, trips to the beach and sand pool, etc. When family visited, we made trips to all the "hot tourist" attractions. Regular stops were Williamsburg, Yorktown, Jamestown, and several local seafood restaurants. Nick's Seafood in Yorktown was one of our favorites. Gerann's parents, Red and Florence, came and brought along her brother Tommy. My sister Joan, husband Clyde, and their youngest son Perry came as well. Their oldest son, Jeff, came on a separate trip; he was in college at Abilene Christian College so when he was off for the summer he made the trip up to Fort Eustis.

Tom and Vickie Arnold and their two children Greg and Valerie (some years later they had another son, Wade) were close friends and remain so today. Tom was in my Transportation Officer Basic Course (TOBC) at Fort Eustis; we were in the same Flight Class, 71-44; we went to Cobra School together, Aircraft Maintenance Officer Course (AMOC) and went to Vietnam on the same plane. Tom is from the panhandle of Oklahoma; he was raised on a farm growing wheat, maze (milo), and corn. Eventually Tom would go back to Oklahoma and pursue his life as a farmer businessman which he is still doing today. They have grown children and grandchildren. Tom also concurrently pursued a military career in the Army Reserve and is a retired Lieutenant Colonel.

John and Cheryl Hirsch were from South Dakota. John and I were together from TOBC to Vietnam just like Tom and me. John remained on active duty for 30 plus years and is a retired Colonel. He and his wife Cheryl are living back in South Dakota. They have grown children and grandchildren as well.

We knew Gary and Judy King at North Georgia College (NGC) before they were married. Some years later, after his active duty years,

Gary and Judy would divorce and Gary is now married to Joyce. They reside in North Carolina. Gary and I also went through training together as I did with Tom and John. However, Gary and I were also together in ROTC Flight Training at NGC. I'm including a story from Gary about his first flight in a Cobra Helicopter as an addendum to this book.

Monk and Glenda Mayhue were one class behind us at NGC. Monk was assigned to Fort Eustis. We spent a lot of time with them sharing meals, bowling, golfing with Monk and other leisure activities. Monk got me involved in the Athletic Officials Association (AOA). We refereed all sports year round and I loved it!

Tom and Lynn Carden were stationed with us at Fort Eustis during my last year and a half on active duty. They were with us at NGC also. We enjoyed meals, dances at the Officer's Club, concerts, etc. with them. Tom did 30 plus years on active duty and is a retired Colonel.

During my years of active duty and my time in the Georgia Army National Guard (31 total years) I was always amazed at the "family atmosphere" that we all shared in the Army. No matter where you served, there would invariably be someone there you had known from a previous assignment, someone that shared a mutual acquaintance with you, someone who had a previous duty station where you had served, etc. Also, it was very common to meet up with fellow NGC Alums along the way. By far the majority of NGC graduates went on to become outstanding officers. Whenever considering assignments, promotions, etc. NGC officers would get "the nod" over most others (West Point being the exception), assuming all things equal.

To say I have been blessed during my life and career would be a gross understatement. I'm including my biographal sketch to act as sort of a "period" to this book project.

12. FELLOW VETERANS' STORIES

*This Story is submitted by Gary King, a fellow Vietnam Veteran and class-*mate from North Georgia College. Gary and I went through our Officer Basic Course at Fort Eustis at approximately the same time. We then were in the same Flight Class, 71-44, Cobra Transition and Aircraft Maintenance Officer Course (AMOC) prior to leaving for Vietnam on the same airplane and then returning eight months later again on the same airplane.

GARY KING

An excellent article by John Cory was published on the subject of POWs and MIAs left behind in Vietnam in the February 1994 issue of The American Spectator. Cory offered a detailed accounting of indisputable evidence that many POWs were left behind in Vietnam. The U.S. Senate ordered an investigation and a committee was appointed, chaired by none other than Senator John Kerry. The long and short of the matter is that, after presentation of all the indisputable evidence to the U.S. Senate, Senator Kerry ordered the destruction of the evidence and the committee was dismissed. I still have my personal copies of the above magazine. The article was reprinted with permission and posted

151

online a few years back, but has since been removed. Since I first read this article in 1994, I've been haunted by the realization that my own personal experiences in Vietnam confirm that there were indeed a large number of men left behind in Vietnam after 1973.

After the Paris Peace Accord was signed on 27 January 1973, the relatively few U.S. Army aviation units left in MR I and II (formerly I Corp and II Corp) began rapidly standing down, sending almost every man home. The 604th Transportation Company was a Direct / General Support Aircraft Maintenance unit in Nha Trang, Vietnam. They were part of the 17th Combat Aviation Command (CAC) in the 1st Aviation Brigade. In the final days of the war, there were about eight officers and enlisted men left in the 604th TC at Camp McDermott, former base camp of the 5th Special Forces just outside Nha Trang Air Force Base. However, we were joined by similar cadres from other aviation units from throughout the regions.

Together we formed a special army rotary wing aviation unit which had a «contingency» mission of POW extractions. The commander of the 17th Combat Aviation Command from Camp Holloway in Pleiku served as our commander. As a 1Lt serving as the Executive Officer (a Major›s slot in this upper echelon aircraft maintenance company), I flew co-pilot with the Commanding Officer of the 604th TC, Major Charlie B. Davis. Each day we spent hours working together to obtain cohesiveness. We flew numerous practice missions out of Nha Trang, each time facing various pre-planned challenges. But practice is all we ever did.

The days passed, and the deadline for the last combat troops to be out of Vietnam drew near. Still, we only flew practice missions as part of a contingency plan. About 26 March 1973, we were ordered to the air base at Nha Trang. Waiting for us there were shiny WWII era C-47 cargo airplanes without markings. The pilots wore blue jeans and civilian shirts. No one had to ask, as we all understood they were Air America, the aviation arm of the CIA. We flew out to Ton Son Nhut

152

airbase in Saigon. On 27 March, I boarded a beautiful orange and white Braniff International Boeing 747 and left Vietnam for home.

Like most, if not all of my brothers, my thoughts during those days were on one thing, going home. The events of the preceding weeks were somewhat mysterious to me, but at the time I chalked it all up to the craziness of the war. At the time, I gave little thought as to exactly why the special aviation unit had been formed in Nha Trang, and why that special unit had stayed in Nha Trang until the very last days of the war.

However, deep down, I always had questions about what happened to the many men who were unaccounted for and potentially left behind in the jungles of Vietnam. John Cory, the American Spectator author, helped me to realize the horrible truths of those last days. Our government knew there were many POWs still in Vietnam as the last combat troops left. The North Vietnamese Army had agreed in Paris to release all American POWs, promising to give the U.S. the locations of POW camps hidden deep in the jungles. The special unit I was a part of would have extracted the POWs. The U.S. Government trusted our enemy to live up to their promises of the Paris Peace Accord, but our enemy remained such to the end. Knowing there was nothing our government would do, the North Vietnamese never revealed the coordinates of the POW camps. They knew that in the days of the anti-Vietnam War sentiment of our nation, our government lacked political capital and would not react militarily. Thus, the cover-up started.

AIR FORCE RESCUE FROM HANOI
BYRON "BONJI" SAURIOL USNR

This mission was inside Route Pack 5 and qualified those of us who flew this mission as members of the Red River Valley Pilots Association ie. The River Rats. For obvious reasons, the membership in this organization is mostly fast mover drivers, but today the Navy A-6 Intruders got involved because this rescue was a joint effort with a Hanoi Alpha strike as the cover.

This mission was my second close to Hanoi and the tension was high. BOWLEG 02 was number two in a flight of four F-4D Phantoms from the 555 TFS who were on a MiG sweep. Just ten days earlier, First Lieutenant John Markle had a MiG kill while flying with the "A" team of MiG hunters from the Triple Nickel at Udorn. This group included soon to be USAF Aces Steve Ritchie, Chuck Debellevue, and Jeff Feinstein. On this day, Markle and his PITTER (WSO), Capt. Jim Williams were down near Hanoi.

We were vectored off the Alpha Strike to assist the Sandys because Ron and I still had the damn SUU-11s on our Intruders and because the Old Man was working overtime to get even with us for what we did last week. Our two-plane strike against a bunch of water buffalo was not going to advance his career in the Navy. Now we were again in Harm's way testing these damn mini guns on a perfectly good bomber. The Old Man should have let the Marines test these things and let us bomb Hanoi again. Now we assist in an Air Force Rescue.

Awards and decorations were a funny thing. A lot of it had to do with how aggressive the awards and decorations officer was. If the missions were not written up well, or not at all, forget it. Ron and I received Navy Commendations for killing cows (ANOTHER SEA STORY) and nothing for going downtown Hanoi alone at night. At the time, Awards and Decorations were the least of our worries. We might get the DFC if some Air Force Second Lieutenant has a good day on his typewriter on this one. Since we were part of a SAR (Search and Rescue) package on a pickup of a MIG killer 35 nm from Hanoi, I guess it rated the DFC whenever the Air Force would write it up. Oh, well, each of us that flew over there knew when we did a good job, and when we were just along for the mission. Suffice to say, I flew better missions that were totally un-rewarded (with medals) and the reward was in the satisfaction of a job well done. (Key the violins!).

Since the flight time to the SAR area was an hour and twenty minutes each way, we had to act quickly once in the area in order to pull off the rescue. Part of the problem with this particular SAR was that just as the Sandy's and Jolly Greens would get ready to attempt a rescue, they would not have a margin of fuel reserve and would have to leave empty handed. We could refuel and stay all day. To circumvent this problem, we launched four ships with 300 gallon center tanks so all would arrive with a good fuel state and would hopefully be able to orchestrate a pickup. This day still took two tankings.

There was considerable amount of resistance in the SAR area as might be expected so close to the North Vietnamese capitol. Virtually everyone was at least fired upon once and both Ron and I took several hits. There were also SA-2s launched in our general direction, but I suspect that our MIG CAP overhead were the ones being targeted. We had several A-6Bs to destroy the SAM sites for the Alpha strike available but we were too busy to enjoy that part of the show.

After six long hours, the mission was called off because they just couldn't get the rescue helicopters in during the remaining daylight. We would be back at first light.

Orders were to return to the ship with the SUU-11 mini guns and the 300 gallon Centerline tank. 15 minutes from FEET WET my Master Caution Light comes on. One of the J-52 / P8bs had to be shut down. Low on fuel, single engine, one mini gun broken, and the other out of 7.62 ammo, the book says "DROP THEM". They don't call them drop tanks for nothing.

Oh well! Another night with the Marines at Da Nang, time to do a little drinking and working up a story to tell the Old Man in the morning. Ok how do I tell him two of his prize miniguns are now in the deepest part of the Yuang River (Red River)? The grunts will be working all night to replace the JU-52 and we will be back at it in the morning.

The next day everybody got their act together and John Markle and Jim Williams were rescued. They spent the night navigating six miles west of the original pick up point in to a little clearing just big enough for the Jolly Green to get in. Later the Air Force did write us up for the assist. I think this was the only reason CAG did not have me put in the Brig. BONJI dropping the Admiral's SU-11s into the Yuan River was not what CAG wanted to tell the Admiral.

BACK HOME SAFE ONE MORE TIME A-6E

After a short break from our Bien Hoa trip, Ron and I went out together yet again. We headed south to Steal Tiger and hit a power station northeast of the Boleyn's Plateau. The political weather up north cancelled the planned additional Hanoi missions, so we were told to move south for new targets on the trail. Still never attacked the docks at Haiphong, we went after the trucks hundreds of miles south of the Russian supply ships one at a time...Next entry in my little logbook would only say "last trip with TREES'.

I was going home in a few days, my flying days were numbered, some floaters in the left eye and night vision going down the tubes. I had orders to go to Washington DC for a two-year tour and an 0-5 slot. I will be lost without Ron Blackwell (TREES), who was KIA by a SAM a month later.

The A-6 worked round the clock in Vietnam, conducting attacks on the targets with a pinpoint accuracy unavailable until the advent of smart bombs first used on the A-6E. A-6Es penetrated the Libyan air

defense in 1986 and were used on a wide range of targets in Operation
Desert Storm. The Intruder was never exported or sold to any other
country in the world because it was an "Any Time, Any Place Attack"
aircraft and had to the ability to do it alone. Just a Pilot and his B/N
could attack any place in the world in any weather, it just wasn't stealth.

COBRA ONE ONE SIX, POWER LOSS
AND GOING DOWN GARY R. KING

On a beautiful day, 22 February of 1972, I was flying co-pilot on my
first training flight in an AH-1G Cobra gunship. We were en route to
Duc Hoa (pronounced "Duck Wah") stage-field at Ft Stewart, Georgia. We had departed from the training school named "Cobra Hall"
at Hunter Army Airfield in Savannah. We were flying at 300' above
I-95 at 160 knots. On our first Cobra flights, we all flew up front in
the co-pilot/gunner's seat. I was awestruck! Sitting in the front seat of
an AH-1 at high airspeed and low altitude felt like sitting on a rocket
with a canopy over me. The cockpit was tight (and I was a whopping
140 lbs!) Everywhere I looked I saw ground rushing by, unless I looked
up, where I saw blue sky. What a rush! We were two or three miles
south of the city when suddenly we lost our engine. The AH-1G only
had one of those!

Instructor Pilot CW3 Eric Young immediately bottomed collective pitch to enter into autorotation, while simultaneously easing back
the cyclic (the "stick.") Cobras can do a "cyclic climb" because of forward airspeed. The collective, the control on the left side of the pilots,
controls the pitch of the main rotor, thus controlling up and down.
Although the collective was bottomed, we popped up to 600' Above
Ground Level with the cyclic climb. At the same time, Mr. Young had
put the aircraft into a steep left bank while giving a "Chuck Yeager"

like mayday call; «Duc Hoa, Cobra one one six, power loss, going down interstate.»

This 23 year old 1LT newbie peter pilot just knew that the three-tour, 2500+ combat flying hours Warrant Officer was showing off. I figured he was using the intercom (not really the radio) to put the fear of God into me on my first Cobra flight. After all, I heard no engine RPM low audio warning. I had been too busy enjoying the ride to notice the master caution and low engine RPM warning lights, and I also had forgotten that Young had pulled the audio warning DC circuit breaker at start-up because he hated to listen to that major irritation.

We were almost back to 300' AGL and had nearly completed a 180 degree turn when the reply came from Duc Hoa stage field, "Ah... Roger one one six. Understand you require assistance?" Gulp! I knew that voice sure wasn't from our intercom. We were in an actual mayday! «Oh God,» I thought!

Mr. "Chuck Yeager" Young replied in a calm, cool voice, "That's affirmative. Cobra one one six is power loss and Going Down interstate."

Truthfully, I didn't have time to be scared. "You weren't kidding, were you?" I asked on intercom, as trees were rushing by outside my left canopy as the steep-banked turn and fall continued.

«Negative. We›re going in» was the calm reply.

"Anything I can do?" I asked in a nervous kid's voice. "Lock in and look back," he said. "Tell me if there's a gap between cars."

Most military helicopters had a yellow handled seat and shoulder harness manual lock lever beside the pilot and copilot seats. If you knew you were going in, you could lock in manually in case the inertia reel harness system failed on impact. Done! (After all, the engine had failed! What else might fail?)

By this time, we were completing a 360 degree full circle while falling like a rock, but Mr. Young had already started the deceleration maneuver. We had a lot of forward airspeed to kill. In a deceleration or "flair" maneuver, the nose is raised abruptly, which forces even more wind through the main rotor and adds more rotor RPM. Nice to have plenty of rotor RPM as you get close to the ground! At the right moment (timing IS everything!); the collective is pulled, adding pitch to the main rotor. The inertia of the spinning main rotor provides enough power for the rotor to create lift, and the chopper eases gently to the ground...IF everything was done just right!

In Cobra gunships, the co-pilot sits front seat. He has a very small instrument panel in front of him and a flat black cowling below the front canopy. The gun sight is mounted on the right front. Otherwise he is completely surrounded by Plexiglas. He's also the main gunner. He can see everywhere (as we used to say, "Fat, dumb, and happy.")

On the other hand, the pilot sits rear seat behind a large panel with instruments and stub wing weapon system controls. There's a rocket/ gun sight on top of the panel. He can't see squat unless the aircraft is nose level or low!

In a nose up attitude, such as deceleration, the Cobra's pilot must continuously look out the sides of the canopy, looking forward and down to see where he's going. He sees nothing but panel by looking straight forward, and he doesn't dare try to look back! (At night it gets more interesting, as the Plexiglas reflects the dim red lights of the instruments.)

My job was to look back from the right front and to try to help Young judge where the cars were vs. where we were about to be. We were nose high, and now fully aligned with I-95 South. As I looked back, my stomach turned. There was a blue car behind us. We would soon meet! "There's a blue car coming right up under us!" "God help us," I prayed.

"I'm committed! We have no power!" Young said, as he lowered the nose, bringing us level with our interstate highway/ runway and at the same time pulling pitch with the collective. Suddenly, we were skidding smoothly on the concrete! Cobras have skids, but it felt like this one had wheels! It was like a perfect fixed wing landing! Somehow the man in the blue car saw us and braked hard. We passed right over him! Others behind him were also able to stop.

"Pop your canopy, roll out, and stop the cars!" Young barked as we were still sliding on the concrete. I literally rolled out my left canopy just as we stopped. My head jerked violently just before my boots hit the pavement. I had forgotten to unplug the ICS (radio/intercom) chord to my flight helmet (duh!) It was unplugged now! As I ran to the rear of the AC, I was taking off my flight jacket and turning it inside out. The day-glow orange jacket became my warning flag as I waved it at cars which were bearing down on us at 70+ mph!

When an aviator is in trouble, he has friends. Ask any pilot. Everyone out there does what they can to help. Army aviators are an extremely close bunch. They think nothing of risking their own lives to save the lives of their brothers. I don't mean that as a brag. That's just the way it is. Ask any Vietnam combat vet.

As I was waving my jacket and praying, I heard a beautiful sound. I looked up to see a flight of Cobra gunships racing north 20 feet above I-95 with landing and search lights blinking on and off. Glory to God! Cars were going everywhere, but not a one crashed!

Young had put Cobra 116 in the center of I-95 South, just past an exit ramp! I simply ran around the gunship and detoured traffic off the interstate. As a couple of UH-1 Hueys set down behind Cobra 116, the Georgia State Patrol arrived. One of those Hueys was full of aircraft maintenance guys. The other was our ride back to Cobra Hall. Young went straight to his commander. I went to my classroom, then straight home, where I fell on my face in the floor and thanked Almighty God for His mercy.

This was one of a dozen or so times God saw fit to keep me here. Even so, I was not faithful to Him for many wasted years of my life.

God has forgiven me for those wasted years. My prayer is that God will use this piece of clay in the way He chooses, and I will ever be faithful to do His will for the remainder of my life. (Since I first composed this story in a Word Document a year or so ago, God has twice again spared me in life-threatening situations! Thank you, Lord!)

Gary King—RVN radio call sign "Highlander One"

"Call unto me, and I will answer thee, and shew thee great and mighty things, which thou knowest not."

—Jeremiah 33:3

"But they that wait upon the LORD shall renew their strength; they shall mount up with wings as eagles; they shall run, and not be weary; and they shall walk, and not faint."

—Isaiah 40:31

JIM FLEMING, A REMARKABLE STORY OF A WWII HERO

The Army's 2nd Infantry Division landed on Omaha Beach on D-day +1, June 7, 1944, near St.Laurent sur Mer. After crossing the Aure River to liberate Trevieres on June 10, the 2nd Infantry Division started a trek across France that would take them all the way into Germany.

The infamous Battle of the Bulge would be part of their 303 days of combat. The 2nd Infantry would suffer 3,031 killed in action; another 12,785 wounded and 457 would perish from wounds. Rockdale resident James Fleming landed with the 2nd Infantry Division on Omaha Beach. A buck private at the time, he would be in continuous combat until 88mm shrapnel and frozen feet during the Battle of the Bulge sent him to the sidelines.

Born into a farming family on July 28, 1925, in Kansas City, Mo.,

Fleming called to mind the Great Depression. "It was rough," he said. "And we lived without any luxuries." Fleming was attending a movie with his brother when a news flash on Pearl Harbor was announced over the theater intercom system. "We heard the news, but frankly we were too young to fully understand the consequences." The entire nation soon understood the aftermath.

Fleming graduated from high school in June 1943, turned 18 in July, was drafted in September, and arrived at Camp Blanding, Fla., for basic training the same month. "It was in the middle of nowhere," Fleming said. "But thousands of soldiers were there." Camp Blanding, 50 miles west of St. Augustine, became the fourth largest city in Florida during World War II.

Fleming trained and became a BAR man (Browning Automatic Rifle) and used it exclusively during combat. "It was heavy," he said. "The BAR weighed more than 20 pounds and I carried 20 pounds of ammunition." A BAR team usually consisted of the gunner and an ammo carrier, but Fleming said, "I didn't find out until after I was out of action about a 'team' concept. Shoot, I humped it through basic and most of France by my lonesome."

Granted a 10-day leave before deployment, Fleming boarded a ship at New York's Port of Embarkation with thousands of other soldiers and sailed across the pond to Belfast, Northern Ireland. The 2nd Infantry Division would train extensively for 10 months in Ireland and Wales in preparation for the Invasion of France on June 6, 1944 — D-day.

June 7, 1944 – D-Day +1: The 2nd Infantry Division had been held in reserve for deployment on D +1. "The sea was rough," Fleming said. "We crawled down rope ladders from the big ships to the smaller landing craft. One guy slipped and fell, broke both his legs." Packed like sardines in the landing craft, Fleming and his group landed on Omaha Beach near St. Laurent sur Mer. Fleming said, "It was mass confusion.

The beach was crawling with activity; men didn't know where to go, a German plane buzzed us and strafed the beach; he didn't hit much though."

When asked about the enormous invasion fleet and the tens of thousands of allied aircraft swarming overhead, Fleming said, "Well, to tell you the truth, we didn't care about the ships and planes. We waded in waist high, got to high ground and concentrated on our own safety. A ground pounder just couldn't take it all in."

Asked about his activity with the BAR, Fleming said, "Don't know how many times I fired it the first few days. The BAR lever offered three rates of fire: single shot, burst, and fully automatic. I kept mine on 'burst' to save ammo and get the best results, but as the heavy weapons guy, I was always called up for support."

Replying to a question as to his "scariest moment," Fleming said, "Every day." What he feared the most? "The German 88mm artillery; we hated it. But without a doubt, the most feared weapon we faced was the Maschinengewehr 42." (Machine gun 42). Of the many nicknames for the MG42, "Hitler's Buzz saw" was one, due to the sound it made in combat. Fleming said, "It sounded like ripping cloth. The MG42 fired 1,200 plus rounds per minute. In comparison, my BAR fired 600 rounds per minute."

Assaulting an airport near the town of Brest, Fleming survived a deadly encounter with the MG42. "The 88s forced me out of a hanger so I took cover behind some hedgerows. Then a MG42 opened up on us from a pillbox. A young lieutenant who had been with us two days raised up to take a look... well, his war was over. He survived, but the MG42 ripped his body." Fleming, squad leader Cody, and a fresh replacement were ordered to outflank the pillbox to hopefully silence it. "That didn't work out too well," Fleming said. In tall grass with limited visibility, Fleming got off several rounds at the pillbox but the MG42 quickly returned fire and hit the new replacement. He said, "I heard a

popping sound as the boy hit the ground. He was dead before he fell."
Fleming and his squad leader carried the dead soldier back to friendly
lines, but the MG42 gunner spotted the Americans crossing a road.
"He was about 300 yards away," Fleming said. "I took two rounds in
my legs. Just nicks, though; no big deal." After a brief respite, the 2nd
Infantry Division moved into a defensive position at St. Vith, Belgium,
and entered Germany on October 3. The snow started. Fleming said, "I
remember one day it was 30 degrees; we almost froze to death."

In the middle of one of the worst winters in European history, Hitler launched his Ardennes Offensive, better known as the Battle of the
Bulge. When asked to depict the Battle of the Bulge, Fleming replied,
"Fighting, fighting, nothing but fighting." With more than one million
men (including the Germans) engaged in fierce combat, survival was
the foremost thought. "We were shelled by 88s; German panzer tanks
machine-gunned us and hurled shells at us; their infantry was on the
attack, and we fought for our lives in freezing temperatures without the
benefit of winter clothes." Fleming took shrapnel in his legs, witnessed
air strikes and tank battles, held his ground and did what he had to
do. Wounded twice in two separate battles, he never received a Purple
Heart. The Battle of the Bulge ended Fleming's ordeal of combat. "My
wounds weren't that bad," he said. "But my feet turned black and blue
from the cold. There was still a little color in my feet, but my toes are
numb to this day. Luckily, I still have them."

Fleming was sent back to England. "While I was there, I married
Joyce, my wife of 67 years." (A native of Bristol, England, Joyce passed
last year).

A veteran of heavy combat, James Fleming elected to stay in the
military but decided to join the newly created United States Air Force
in 1947. "I guess I had enough ground pounding," he said. Fleming
retired from the Air Force in 1967 with the rank of Chief Master Sergeant. He'd worn a military uniform for 24 years before serving anoth-

er 21 years with the Army/Air Force Exchange Service. After having a photo taken with his dog Nipper, Fleming asked, "Would you like to see a photo of me and President Truman?" It seems this remarkable man not only knew Harry Truman, but played poker with him on a regular basis at the American Legion Hall in Independence, Missouri, but that's another story.

Pete Mecca is a Vietnam veteran, columnist and freelance writer. Contact Pete at aveteransstory@gmail.com and visit his website ataveteransstory.us.

EXTRA STUFF

Throughout the years I've often said that if you can fly a TH-55 ("Mattel Messerschmitt") and do a side hill landing then you can fly anything! This was the little trainer that we learned to fly at Fort Wolters. I must say learning to hover the TH-55 was perhaps the most difficult thing I've ever learned to do.

ENGINEERING FLIGHT TEST
TH-55A PRIMARY HELICOPTER TRAINER
LIMITED PERFORMANCE EVALUATION

FINAL REPORT

Samuel R. Schwartz

CPT, CE

US ARMY

Project Engineer

Donald P. Wray

MAJ, TC

US ARMY

Project Officer/Pilot

November 1969

DESCRIPTION

4. The TH-55A is a two-place helicopter manufactured by the Hughes Tool Company Aircraft Division. It incorporates a single three bladed, fully-articulated main rotor and a two-bladed, teetering,

1

Anti-torque tail rotor. The seating arrangement is side-by-side facilitating its use as a primary trainer. Power is supplied by a Lycoming H10-360-B1A reciprocating engine with a SL takeoff rating of 180 shaft horsepower (shp) at 2<100 rpm. The helicopter's empty weight is 1006 pounds, and the design grwt is 1670 pounds. The helicopter used during this test program was weighed prior to the start of the tests (app VI). Pertinent dimensions are as follows:

a. Main rotor diameter: 25.29 feet.

b. Overall length (rotors turning): 28.40 feet.

c. Overall width (rotors turning): 25.29 feet.

d. Overall height (struts extended): 8.58 feet.

29. The auto-rotational entry characteristics were examined during the auto-rotational descent performance tests, as well as during simulated engine failures (throttle chops) at speeds up to $V_{N\!E}$. At lower speeds, the aircraft responses were relatively mild when power was lost and collective was lowered. A yaw to the left and a longitudinal trim change requiring aft cyclic control were apparent to the pilot. In addition, right-lateral cyclic control was required. However, at higher airspeeds the longitudinal trim change became more severe; and if pilot reaction was slow, the helicopter could achieve an uncomfortable nose-down attitude. This characteristic is considered to be a deficiency requiring mandatory correction (HQRS 7).

DEFICIENCIES AND SHORTCOMINGS AFFECTING MISSION ACCOMPLISHMENT

34. Mandatory correction of auto-rotational entry characteristics should be made at the earliest possible time (para 29).

35. Correction of the following shortcomings is desirable for improved operation and mission capability:

a. Insufficient cyclic trim control throughout the flight envelope (para 26).

b. Inadequately damped roll/yaw oscillations during flight in turbulent air (para 27).

c. Inadequate operator's manual (para 32).

RECOMMENDATIONS

36. The deficiency, correction of which is mandatory, should be correct-
ed as soon as possible.

37. The shortcomings, correction of which is desirable, should be cor-
rected on a high-priority basis.

NEGOTIATED PEACE AGREEMENT TO
END THE VIETNAM WAR

The document began with the statement that "the United States and all other countries respect the independence, *sovereignty,* unity, and *territorial integrity* of Vietnam as recognized by the *1954 Geneva Agreements on Vietnam".* The inclusion of this provision was a victory for the communist side of the negotiations by allowing that the war was not a foreign aggression against South Vietnam. The main military and political provisions of the agreement were:

1. Beginning on 27 January 1973 at midnight, *Greenwich Mean Time*—in Saigon time, 08:00 on 28 January—there would be an in-place *ceasefire.* North and South Vietnamese forces were to hold their locations. They were permitted to resupply military materials to the extent necessary to replace items consumed in the course of the truce.

2. Once the ceasefire is in effect, U.S. troops (along with other non-Vietnamese soldiers) would begin to withdraw, with withdrawal to be complete within 60 days. Simultaneously, U.S. *prisoners of war* would be released and allowed to return home.

The parties to the agreement agreed to assist in *repatriating* the remains of the dead.

3. There would be negotiations between the two South Vietnamese parties—Saigon and the *Vietcong*—towards a political settlement that would allow the South Vietnamese people to "decide themselves the political future of South Viet-Nam through genuinely free and democratic general elections under international supervision."

4. Reunification of Vietnam was to be "carried out step by step through peaceful means".

5. If South Vietnam required any military hardware to defend itself against any North Vietnam aggression, the United States agreed to provide replacement aid to the South Vietnam on a piece-by-piece, one-to-one replacement basis.

27 JANUARY 1973

The United States, South Vietnam, Viet Cong, and North Vietnam formally sign "An Agreement Ending the War and Restoring Peace in Vietnam" in Paris. Due to South Vietnam's unwillingness to recognize the Viet Cong's Provisional Revolutionary Government, all references to it were confined to a two-party version of the document signed by North Vietnam and the United States—the South Vietnamese were presented with a separate document that did not make reference to the Viet Cong government. This was part of Saigon's long-time refusal to recognize the Viet Cong as a legitimate participant in the discussions to end the war.

The settlement included a cease-fire throughout Vietnam. It addition, the United States agreed to the withdrawal of all U.S. troops and advisors (totaling about 23,700) and the dismantling of all U.S. bases within 60 days. In return, the North Vietnamese agreed to release all U.S. and other prisoners of war.

Both sides agreed to the withdrawal of all foreign troops from Laos and Cambodia and the prohibition of bases in and troop movements through these countries. It was agreed that the DMZ at the 17th Parallel would remain a provisional dividing line, with eventual reunification of the country "through peaceful means." An international control commission would be established made up of Canadians, Hungarians, Poles, and Indonesians, with 1,160 inspectors to supervise the agreement. According to the agreement, South Vietnamese President Nguyen Van Thieu would continue in office pending elections. Agreeing to "the South Vietnamese People's right to self-determination," the North Vietnamese said they would not initiate military movement across the DMZ and that there would be no use of force to reunify the country.

Footnote: The last U.S. serviceman to die in combat in Vietnam, Lt. Col. William B. Nolde, was killed by an artillery shell at An Loc, 60 miles northwest of Saigon, only 11 hours before the truce went into effect.

PRESIDENT NIXON

Nixon had secretly promised Thiêu that he would use *airpower* to support the Saigon government should it be necessary. During his confirmation hearings in June 1973, *Secretary of Defense James Schlesinger* was sharply criticized by some senators after he stated that he would recommend resumption of U.S. bombing in North Vietnam if North Vietnam launched a major offensive against South Vietnam, but by August 15, 1973, 95% of American troops and their allies had left Vietnam (both North and South) as well as *Cambodia* and *Laos* under the *Case-Church Amendment.* The amendment, which was approved by the U.S. Congress in June 1973, prohibited further U.S. military activity in Vietnam, Laos, and Cambodia unless the president secured Congressional approval in advance. However, during this time, Nixon was being driven from office due to the *Watergate scandal,* which led to his resignation in 1974. When the North Vietnamese began *their final offensive* early in 1975, U.S. Congress refused to appropriate additional military assistance for South Vietnam, citing strong opposition to the war by Americans and the loss of American equipment to the North by retreating Southern forces. Thiêu subsequently resigned, accusing the U.S. of betrayal in a TV and radio address

Saigon fell to the North Vietnamese army supported by Viet Cong units on April 30, 1975. Schlesinger had announced early in the morning of April 29 the beginning of *Operation Frequent Wind,* which entailed the evacuation of the last U.S. diplomatic, military and civilian personnel from Saigon via helicopter, which was completed in the early morning hours of April 30. Not only did North Vietnam conquer South Vietnam, but the communists were also victorious in Cambodia when the *Khmer Rouge* captured *Phnom Penh* on April 17, as were the *Pathet Lao* in Laos successful in capturing *Vientiane* on December 2. Like Saigon, U.S. civilian and military personnel were evacuated from Phnom Penh, U.S. diplomatic presence in Vientiane was significantly downgraded, and the number of remaining U.S. personnel was severely reduced.

WHEN DID THE VIETNAM WAR START?

French colonialism in Vietnam lasted more than six decades. By the late 1880s France controlled Vietnam, Laos and Cambodia, which it referred to as *Indochina Francais* (French Indochina). Indochina became one of France's most lucrative colonial possessions. It was part of a French empire that spanned northern and western Africa, as well as islands in the Caribbean and the Pacific. To justify their imperialism, the French developed their own principle called the *mission civilisatrice* (or 'civilizing mission'). It was, in effect, a French form of the English 'white man's burden'. French imperialists claimed it was their responsibility to colonize undeveloped regions in Africa and Asia, to introduce modern political ideas, social reforms, industrial methods and new technologies. Without European intervention these places would remain backward, uncivilized and impoverished.

By the 1930s Indochina was supplying 60,000 tons of rubber each year, five per cent of all global production. The French also constructed factories and built mines to tap into Vietnam's deposits of coal, tin and zinc. Most of this material was sold abroad as exports. Most of the profits lined the pockets of French capitalists, investors and officials.

The workers on plantations in French Indochina were known as 'coolies' (a derogatory term for Asian laborers). They worked long hours in debilitating conditions, for wages that were pitifully small. Some were paid in rice rather than money. The working day could be as long as 15 hours, without breaks or adequate food and fresh water. French colonial laws prohibited corporal punishment but many officials and overseers used it anyway, beating slow or reluctant workers. Malnutrition, dysentery and malaria were rife on plantations, especially those producing rubber. It was not uncommon for plantations to have several workers die in a single day. Conditions were particularly poor on the plantations owned by French tire manufacturer Michelin. In the 20 years between the two world wars, one Michelin-owned plantation recorded 17,000 deaths. Vietnamese peasant farmers who remained outside the plantations were subject to the *corvee*, or unpaid labor. Introduced in 1901, the *corvee* required male peasants of adult age to complete 30 days of unpaid work on government buildings, roads, dams and other infrastructure.

1. The French colonization of Vietnam began in earnest in the 1880s and lasted six decades. The French justified their imperialism with a 'civilizing mission', a pledge to develop backward nations.

2. In reality, French colonialism was chiefly driven by economic interests. French colonists were interested in acquiring land, exploiting labor, exporting resources and making profit. Vietnamese land was seized by the French and collectivized into large rice and rubber plantations. Local farmers were forced to labor on these plantations in difficult and dangerous conditions.

3. The French also imposed a range of taxes on the local population and implemented monopolies on critical goods, such as opium, salt and alcohol.

4. French colonizers were relatively few in number so were assisted by Francophile collaborators among the Vietnamese people. These collaborators assisted in the administration and exploitation of French Indochina.

In early 1954, the French Army was encamped at Dien Bien Phu, a heavily fortified base located deep in a valley and near communications links on the Laotian border. By mid-March, it was clear that the French were struggling under a Viet Minh siege and that only outside intervention in the form of fresh troops or airstrikes could save them. Though President Eisenhower was determined to prevent a communist victory in Vietnam, the U.S. Congress and officials in the Administration were equally determined not to intervene unless they could do so as a part of a larger coalition. Britain and other members of NATO declined to participate in rescuing what they thought was a lost cause. Dien Bien Phu fell in May, and the French retreated from Vietnam.

In the wake of the French defeat, the French and Vietnamese, along with representatives from the United States and China, met in Geneva in mid-1954 to discuss the future of Indochina. They reached two agreements. First, the French and the Viet Minh agreed to a cease-fire and a temporary division of the country along the 17th parallel. French forces would remain in the South, and Ho Chi Minh's forces would control the North. The second agreement promised that neither the North nor the South would join alliances with outside parties, and called for general elections in 1956. Laos and Cambodia were to remain neutral.

The United States did not sign the second agreement, establishing instead its own government in South Vietnam. As the French pulled out, the United States appointed Ngo Dinh Diem to lead South Vietnam. Like Bao Dai, Diem was an unpopular choice in Vietnam as he had waited out the nationalist struggle against France abroad. Diem had also collaborated with the Japanese occupation, but his Catholicism appealed to the Western powers. The United States also supported the formation of the Southeast Asia Treaty Organization, designed to respond if there was an armed attack on any nation in the region.

U. S. INVOLVEMENT

Some view *December 1956* when Hanoi authorized a low-level insurgency in South Vietnam as the start date, while some consider *September 26, 1959* when the first battle between the North communist and South Vietnamese forces occurred. Some argue it should be on *June 8, 1956* when U.S. Air Force Technical Sergeant Richard B. Fitzgibbon Jr. became the first American to die in the conflict. Others insist that the conflict only started after the first U.S. bombing operation in Vietnam called Operation Pierce Arrow on *August 5, 1964* in retaliation for strikes against U.S. destroyers during the *Gulf of Tonkin incident.*

On November 06, 1998, after an extensive review of qualifying criteria, the Department of Defense officially lists American deaths in Vietnam from November 1, 1955 which, in other words, could be now considered as the start date of the Vietnam War or *Vietnam conflict,* to be precise. That was the day when the Military Assistance Advisory Group (MAAG) Vietnam was created from the MAAG Indochina, which had been established since 1950 under President Harry Truman, to support South Vietnam in their war against the North Vietnamese communists

ADDITIONAL HISTORICAL FACTS
ABOUT THE VIETNAM WAR

On March 8, 1965, the first American combat troops – the 9th Marine Expeditionary Brigade – waded ashore at China Beach north of Da Nang. There had already been limited U.S. Naval action, and the bombing of North Vietnam had commenced. There were also 23,000 military advisors already on the ground as of March 8th.

Under President Lyndon B. Johnson (1963-1968), US intervention mushroomed both militarily and politically. Johnson asked for a resolution expressing U.S. determination to support freedom and protect peace in Southeast Asia. Congress responded with the Tonkin Gulf Resolution, expressing support for "all necessary measures" the President might take to repel armed attacks against US forces and prevent further aggression.

Army Chief of Staff Harold K. Johnson estimated in 1965 that victory would require as many as 700,000 troops for up to five years.

Commandant of the Marine Corps Wallace Greene made a similar estimate on troop levels. As President Johnson incrementally escalated the war, neither man made his views known to the president or Congress. President Johnson made a concerted effort to conceal the costs and consequences of Vietnam from the public, but such duplicity required the passive consent of America's generals.

The brutal murder of the president of South Vietnam, Ngo Dinh Diem, and his powerful brother and adviser, Ngo Dinh Nhu, on November 2, 1963, was a major turning point in the war in Vietnam. Up until the deaths of the Ngo brothers, the United States had been 'advising' the government of South Vietnam in its war against the Viet Cong and their benefactors, the government of North Vietnam. At the time, the United States had 16,000 troops in South Vietnam training the ARVN forces and even going so far as to accompany them on helicopter-borne raids deep into enemy territory. American casualties were beginning to mount, and images of the dead were being broadcast on stateside network television.

In the wake of the assassinations, American policy toward the war in Vietnam changed dramatically. The murder of President John F. Kennedy almost three weeks later placed a new head of state in the White House. Lyndon B. Johnson carried on his predecessor's Vietnam policies until 1964, when American participation in the war dramatically increased. A series of corrupt generals ruled Saigon while American forces would eventually reach the 500,000 mark.

Year	American	SVN	Aust.	Korea	New Zeal	Philip	Thai
1959	760	243000	--	--	--	--	--
1960	900	243000	--	--	--	--	--
1961	3205	243000	--	--	--	--	--
1962	11300	243000	--	--	--	--	--
1963	16300	243000	--	--	--	--	--
1964	23300	514000	198	200	30	20	--
1965	184300	642500	1560	20620	120	70	20
1966	385300	735900	4530	25570	160	2060	240
1967	485600	798700	6820	47830	530	2020	2200
1968	536100	820000	7660	50000	520	1580	6000
1969	475200	897000	7670	48870	550	190	11570
1970	334600	968000	6800	48450	440	70	11570
1971	156800	1046250	2000	45700	100	50	6000
1972	24200	1048000	130	36790	50	50	40
1973	50						

"KILLING FIELDS" IN CAMBODIA

Pol Pot Regime and Khmer Rouge in Cambodia killed between 1.5 million and 3 million Cambodians between 1975 and 1979.

END OF VIETNAM WAR

U.S. Congress funded South Vietnam in fiscal year 1973 at $2.8 billion; in 1975 they cut it to $300 million

It took only 55 days for the NVA to defeat the ARVN; Saigon fell on April 30, 1975

EPILOGUE

Well, that's my story, or at least part of it. A lot has happened in the world and in my life since my time in Vietnam. That immediately prompts me to begin thinking about a possible second book. As I stated in the Prologue, my intention was to get my story on paper so that my family and friends would have something to remember me by. I believe I've accomplished that objective.

This entire process has been a learning experience for me. One of the things I wanted to do was mention by name a number of people that had an influence on me as I negotiated the various "hurdles" in my formative years and as I began my career, particularly in the military. My father, Forrest Anderson Blanton, and my mother, Eura Lee (Bell) Blanton, of course both had a great deal of influence on me as I grew up and on into my adult years.

As I stated in other parts of the book, it's dangerous to mention names because invariably you will forget somebody. Nevertheless, here are a few other names that I may not have mentioned earlier. These folks helped me in my career; some to a greater extent than others but they all influenced me in a positive way and were encouragers, supporters, and sometimes confidants. Some I worked for and others worked for me. During my active duty years: Larry Hanson, Dennis Burke, Ira Silverman, Jerry Childers, Marshall Eubanks, Dale Wells, and Tom

Wolf. During my career with the Georgia Army National Guard: W. H. Ashburn, Phillip Stephens, T. J. Jaynes, Joe Pierson, David Young, Andy Durden, Dick Stokes, Greg Edwards, David Clute, Ralph Allen, Robert Tadlock, Leslie Groover, Jimmy Fletcher, Joel Seymour, Steve Reece, David Dumas, Eddie Standard, Russ Lapanna, Stu Drake, Perry Carter, Jeff Farrell, Danny Stone, Kelvin Newsome and Larry Ross. During my Teaching and Coaching Career: Jack Purcell, Shirley Pittman, Virginia Boswell, Evans Acree, Thomas Glanton, Jerry Aldrige, Ben Harris, Jon DeVetter, Dan Spear, Jean Austin, Paul Jones, Ken Mitchell, Irven Smith, Steve Smith, and Tim Bice.

Many others were important in my life in various ways, either Church, Gideon Ministry, neighbors, friends, or professional association. Here are a few of those: Reid Callaway (a real Prayer Warrior), Frances Thompson (my first Sunday School Teacher at Rutledge Baptist Church), James Melvin Brewer, Raymond Gilbert, Mike Huff, Ray Rousseau, and Jimmy Thompson. Of course, once this book goes to press I will, no doubt, remember many others that I should have mentioned. The fact is, I've been blessed during my life with numerous friends who have helped me in various ways with their encouraging words, sound advice, influence with others, and most of all with their prayers.

At this writing we received some awesome news from our youngest son Ben and his wife Sarah. They are expecting their first baby which will be our tenth grandbaby! The blessings just keep coming! Thank you for reading my story and I pray for God's blessings on you and your family.

PHOTOGRAPHS

Trying on my Dress Blues at NGC with my TC Brass and ROTC Flight Wings

Our Wedding Party on June 6, 1970

Me and Bob Stein on 23 April 1970 during the Gainesville-Dahlonega Memorial Run

Scott Shemwell followed me the last half mile with the fire extinguisher!

Family Day at Fort Wolters

If you can fly a TH-55 then you can fly anything!

TH-55 ("Mattel Messerschmitt")

Class 71-44 Section A-1 Fort Wolters

187

Class 71–44 Section A-2 Fort Wolters

Flight School Fort Rucker, Gerann pinning my wings on at Graduation

Robert & Inez came to my Flight School Graduation

Cobra Transition at Hunter Army Airfield March 1972

First picture in Vietnam, Me and Beetle in Saigon

David Bailey in his office at MACV HDQS, Saigon

Latrine, my Hooch Maid, my room

Final Approach to a dock landing

Survival Vest

Typical Firebase, note the three landing pads at bottom center

Me at Firebase Shroder

Super Shaft Six, my office at the Maintenance Hangar

Me & Old Man, MAJ Jerry Childers

Super Shaft 6 Jeep

ARVN NVA US VC - March 1973

Tony Dal Pozzo's grave. He was killed on Day One of the Peace Treaty!

This was the last six left in my 40-man platoon just days prior to our leaving

Coming Home March 1973, VC & NVA Observers

Gary King and Me stopover in Hawaii on way home!

Dale Wells, Me, Brother Robert in Del City 1973

Williamsburg Summer 1973. Gary & Judy King, Vickie & Tom Arnold, Me & Gerann

Summer '73, Tom & Vickie Arnold, Cheryl & John Hirsch

Me, Jerry Childers, John Harris at AAHF Summer 2017

Flight Class Reunion Oct '17

July 2017 We've added one and one on the way

Me & Gerann in Paris October '17

Jesse, Robin & Family

Chris, Laura & Family

Patrick & Stephanie with Jackson

Sarah & Ben

ABOUT THE AUTHOR

STEVEN E. BLANTON
BRIGADIER GENERAL (RETIRED)
GEORGIA ARMY NATIONAL GUARD
COLONEL (RETIRED) U.S. ARMY

General Steven E. Blanton was born in Atlanta, Georgia. He entered the Army in October of 1970 as a newly commissioned Second Lieutenant out of North Georgia College. After completing his officer basic course in Transportation at Ft. Eustis, Virginia, he was assigned to the 355th Heavy Helicopter Company as a Technical Supply Officer. In April of 1971, General Blanton was selected for the Officer Rotary Wing Aviator Course at Ft. Wolters, Texas and Ft. Rucker, Alabama. He received his Aviator Wings in February of 1972 and then completed Cobra Transition in March at Hunter Army Airfield in Savannah where he learned to fly the AH-1G gunship. After completing the Aircraft Maintenance Officer Course at Ft. Eustis, Virginia, General Blanton was assigned to the 18th Corps Aviation Company (CAC) which was part of the 1st Aviation Brigade, in the Republic of Vietnam. While in Vietnam, he flew over 300 hours of combat support missions and served as a platoon leader in the 18th CAC.

Upon his return from Vietnam, General Blanton was assigned to the 155th Transportation Company at Ft. Eustis, Virginia. He served as the Executive Officer of that company and later as the Training Officer for the 10th Transportation Battalion. In August of 1974, General Blanton ended his active duty time and received his Honorable Discharge in April of 1976.

In March of 1983, General Blanton entered the Georgia Army National Guard after a nine-year break in service. His first assignment was as a platoon leader and later as executive officer of the 201st Maintenance Company. Later assignments included serving as the S-3 Operations Officer and S-4 Logistics Officer of the 110th Maintenance Battalion. General Blanton served as Commanding Officer of the 277th Maintenance Company on two different occasions for a total of 60 months. His varied assignments include two overseas deployments, Ecuador in September of 1987 where he served as Base Camp Commander for a humanitarian road building project and Germany in February of 1993 where he led the 277th Maintenance Company in a retrograde mission preparing excess equipment for shipment to emerging democratic countries in Europe. General Blanton served as Battalion Commander for the 201st Supply and Service Battalion from Aug 2004 to Feb 2006 and then as Commander of the 201st Regional Support Group from Feb 2006 to Aug 2007. As Commander of the 201st S & S Battalion, General Blanton led an 800 soldier task force in support of relief operations in the aftermath of hurricane Katrina.

General Blanton taught school for a total of 24 years at Rutledge Academy, Nathaniel Greene Academy, Newton High School, and Eastside High School. He coached high school sports; football, basketball, and track for a total of eight years. General Blanton served as a Rutledge City Councilman from 1978 to 1984 and as a volunteer fireman for fifteen years. General Blanton resigned from his position as Related Vocational Instruction Coordinator at Eastside High School in June of 2000 to accept a fulltime position as Superintendent of the Georgia Maneuver Area Training and Equipment Site (GA MATES) at Fort Stewart, Georgia. In this position, General Blanton supervised a workforce of 150 military technicians and was charged with the responsibility of maintaining equipment readiness of combat systems for two mechanized infantry brigades.

General Blanton was next assigned as the Equipment Readiness Supervisor for the Directorate of Logistics. In this position, General Blanton was responsible for readiness reporting of combat equipment for all Georgia Army National Guard Units. General Blanton was promoted in July of 2004 to the position of Surface Maintenance Manager for the Georgia Army National Guard. His maintenance division of 350 technicians and 14 shops was responsible for equipment readiness for all units in the Georgia Army National Guard. During General Blanton's tenure, equipment readiness consistently remained at high levels of 90% or better during a time of increased OPTEMO due to the Global War on Terror.

The National Guard Bureau recognized General Blanton's maintenance division as being "forward thinking" due to the development of a twenty-year maintenance plan for the Georgia Army National Guard under his leadership. This twenty-year plan will ensure a high state of equipment readiness for many years to come. General Blanton retired from military service on 28 Aug 2008, culminating 31 years in uniform. General Blanton retired from full time employment on 30 Sep 2010 with the Military Personnel Services Company as Program

Support Manager for the Georgia Committee of ESGR (Employer Support for the Guard and Reserve).

General Blanton is active in his church, Rutledge Baptist, where he has served in several capacities, including Sunday School Director and Teacher, Treasurer, and Trustee. He was ordained as a deacon in 1981. Additionally, he has been actively involved in the Gideon Ministry since 1985 where he has had the opportunity to serve as a church speaker delivering stewardship reports in numerous churches throughout Georgia.

His awards and decorations include the Legion of Merit, Bronze Star for Meritorious Service, Air Medal with "V" device for Valor, six Air Medals, two Meritorious Service Medals, Army Commendation Medal, Joint Defense Service Medal, four Army Achievement Medals, Vietnam Service Ribbon, Vietnam Campaign Ribbon, Vietnamese Cross of Gallantry with Palm, National Defense Service Medal, and the Army Aviator Badge. His state awards include the Georgia Meritorious Service Medal, Georgia Humanitarian Service Ribbon, Mississippi Humanitarian Service Ribbon, and State Active Duty Ribbon.

General Blanton and his wife Gerann reside in Social Circle, Georgia. Gerann is a retired middle school math teacher and retired choir director at Rutledge Baptist Church. They have three sons, a daughter, and nine grandchildren. Chris, 43, and wife Laura reside in Winder, GA where Chris is the Minister of Music at Winder First Baptist Church; they have an eleven-year old son Stephen, a eight-year old daughter Abigail, six-year old son, Samuel, four-year old son, Alexander and a one-year old daughter, Victoria. Jesse, 42, is a Lieutenant Colonel in the US Army, a three-time Iraqi war veteran and two-time veteran of Operation Enduring Freedom in Afghanistan. Jesse, wife Robin, daughter Lauren, 12, son Joshua, 10, and daughter Georgia, 5, reside in Wiesbaden, Germany where Jesse is assigned to U.S. Army Europe. Ben, 37, and wife Sarah currently reside in Covington, Georgia. Ben is pursuing a career in real estate. He graduated from the University of Georgia, Terry Business College with a BS Degree in Business Management. Ben and Sarah are expecting their first baby at the end of 2019 (our tenth grandchild!) Stephanie, 34, husband, Patrick Barnes and son Jackson, two years old, reside in Sugar Hill, Georgia. Stephanie is a Registered Nurse and Doctor Barnes is an Orthodontist.

At this writing, I am soon to be 71 years old (August 29, 2019) and Lord willing I have many more years ahead to enjoy retirement with Gerann and watch our family grow and prosper. We are hopeful that The Lord will bless us with even more grandbabies in the coming years. To steal a line from one of my favorite Christmas movies, *"I've had a Wonderful Life"*!

CPSIA information can be obtained
at www.ICGtesting.com
Printed in the USA
LVHW080759281019
635534LV00003B/140/P